DORLING KINDERSLEY DK EYEWITNESS BOOKS

MATTER

Open and shut mold for making apothecaries' vials (19th century)

Metals produced by electrolysis (mid 19th century)

Crookes's thallium compounds and notebook (1860s)

Measuring cylinder (19th century)

Model of adenovirus (20th century)

Ammonium dichromate crystals

Bunsen burner (19th century)

Graphite

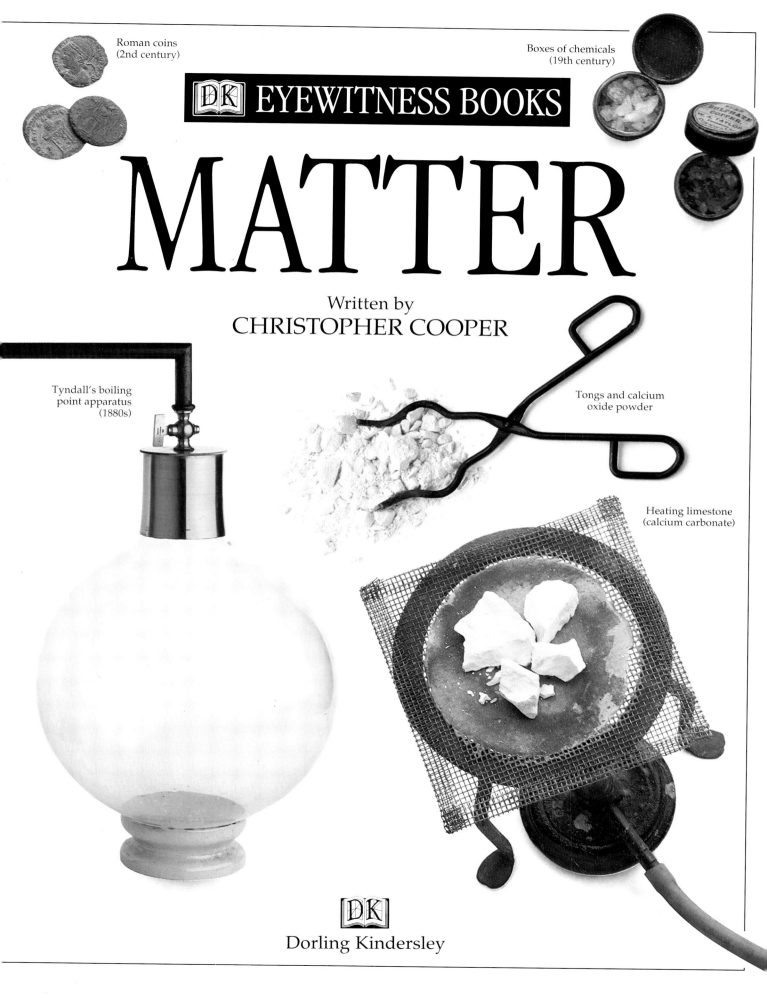

Roman coins
(2nd century)

Boxes of chemicals
(19th century)

DK EYEWITNESS BOOKS

MATTER

Written by
CHRISTOPHER COOPER

Tyndall's boiling
point apparatus
(1880s)

Tongs and calcium
oxide powder

Heating limestone
(calcium carbonate)

DK
Dorling Kindersley

Boxes of chemicals (19th century)

Thermometer of
Lyons (18th century)

Ancient
Egyptian
mirror

Items from a box of flame test
equipment (19th century)

DK

Dorling Kindersley

**LONDON, NEW YORK, AUCKLAND, DELHI, JOHANNESBURG,
MUNICH, PARIS and SYDNEY**

For a full catalog, visit

DK www.dk.com

Project editor Sharon Lucas
Designer Heather McCarry
DTP manager Joanna Figg-Latham
Production Eunice Paterson
Managing editor Josephine Buchanan
Senior art editor Neville Graham
Special photography Dave King
Editorial consultant Alan Morton, Science Museum, London
Special consultant Jack Challoner
US editor Charles A. Wills
US consultant Harvey B. Loomis

This Eyewitness ® Book has been conceived by
Dorling Kindersley Limited and Editions Gallimard

© 1992 Dorling Kindersley Limited
This edition © 2000 Dorling Kindersley Limited
First American edition, 1999

Published in the United States by
Dorling Kindersley Publishing, Inc.
95 Madison Avenue
New York, NY 10016
2 4 6 8 10 9 7 5 3 1

Dorling Kindersley books are available at special discounts for bulk purchases
for sales promotions or premiums. Special editions, including personalized
covers, excerpts of existing guides, and corporate imprints can be created in
large quantities for specific needs. For more information, contact Special
Markets Dept., Dorling Kindersley Publishing, Inc., 95 Madison Ave.,
New York, NY 10016; Fax: (800) 600-9098

Library of Congress Cataloging-in-Publication Data
Cooper, Christopher.
Matter / written by Christopher Cooper.
p. cm. — (Eyewitness Books)
Includes index.
Summary: Examines the elements that make up the physical world
and the properties and behavior of different kinds of matter.
1. Matter—Constitution—Juvenile literature. 2. Matter—Properties—Juvenile
literature. 3. Atoms—Juvenile literature. 4. Molecules—Juvenile literature.
[1. Matter. 2. Atoms. 3. Molecules.] I. Title. II. Series.
QC173. 16. C66   2000   530—dc20   92-6928
                                                  CIP
                                                  AC

ISBN 0-7894-6173-0 (pb)
ISBN 0-7894-5580-3 (hc)

Color reproduction by Colourscan, Singapore
Printed in China by Toppan Printing Co. (Shenzhen) Ltd.

Bunsen
burner
(1872)

Contents

Molecular model and components (19th century)

What is matter?

Everything found everywhere in the universe – from the farthest star to the smallest speck of dust – is made of matter in an incredible variety of forms. About 200 years ago heat was regarded by many scientists as being a special sort of matter. But now it is known that heat is simply the motion of tiny particles of matter (pp. 38-39). Sound, too, is a certain type of movement of matter. Forms of energy such as radiation (for example, light, radio waves, and X-rays) are generally regarded as not being matter, though they are very closely linked to it. All the different kinds of matter have one thing in common – mass. This is the amount of material in any object, and shows itself as resistance to being moved. A truck, for example, has more mass and is much harder to move than a toy car. Every piece of matter in the universe attracts every other piece of matter. The amount of matter is important – a large piece attracts other matter more strongly than a small piece.

A CONTAINED UNIVERSE
This terrarium is a microcosm of the living world. It contains the three states of matter – solids (pp. 12-13), liquids (pp. 18-19), and gases (pp. 20-21), as well as interesting substances found in the world of matter.

THE LIVING WORLD
All living matter (pp. 42-43) can organize itself into intricate forms and behave in complicated ways. It was once thought that matter in living things was controlled by a "vital principle," a sort of ghostly force. But now scientists think that living and nonliving matter obey the same laws.

Plants grow upward to reach the light

MIXING AND SEPARATING MATTER
Gravel, sand, and water can be made into a mixture (pp. 26-27), and can easily be separated afterwards. Each of these materials is made of other substances that are more strongly combined and very hard to separate. Water, for example, is a combination of the gases hydrogen and oxygen. Such a close combination is called a chemical compound (pp. 26-27).

A mixture of gravel, sand, and water

METALLIC MATTER
Metals (pp. 16-17) are found in rocks called ores. Pure metals are rare, and usually they have to be separated from their ores. Once separated, they are often combined with other materials to form alloys – mixtures of metals and other substances.

Lead is a metal which looks solid, but flows extremely slowly over decades

SOLUTIONS AND COLLOIDS
Substances can often dissolve in a liquid or solid. They form
solutions – they are mixed very thoroughly with the liquid
or solid, breaking up into groups of a few atoms, or even
into single atoms (these are the smallest normally existing
particles of matter, pp. 34-35). A colloid (pp. 24-25)
consists of larger particles of matter that are
suspended in a solid, liquid, or gas.

Glass is transparent matter

THE WORLD OF GASES
When the particles of a substance become
separated from each other, the substance
becomes a gas. It has no shape of its own,
but expands to fill any space available.
Air (largely a mixture of nitrogen and
oxygen) was the first gas to be
recognized. It was many centuries
before scientists realized that there
are other gases as well as air. This
was because gases tend to look
similar – they are mostly
colorless and transparent.

*Condensation is caused
by molecules of water
vapor cooling and
turning into a liquid*

LIQUID MATTER
Liquids, like gases, consist
of matter that can flow,
but unlike gases, they
settle at the bottom of
any container. Nearly all
substances are liquids at
certain temperatures. The
most important liquid for
living creatures is water.
Most of the human body
is made up of water. It
forms the bulk of human
blood, which transports
dissolved foodstuffs and
waste products around
the body.

*Water contains
dissolved oxygen
and carbon dioxide
gases from the air*

*This butterfly is made
of some of the millions
of varieties of living
matter on earth*

SOLID SHAPES
The metal and glass
(pp. 24-25) of this terrarium
could not act as a container
for plant and animal
specimens if they did not
keep a constant shape.
Matter that keeps a definite
shape is called solid.
However, most solids will
lose their shape if they are
heated sufficiently, turning
into a liquid or a gas.

*Solids such as rock
keep a definite shape*

Ideas of the Greeks

ANCIENT GREEK PHILOSOPHERS vigorously debated the nature of matter and concluded that behind its apparent complexity the world was really very simple. Thales (about 600 BC) suggested that all matter was made of water. Empedocles (5th century BC) believed that all matter consisted of four basic substances, or elements – earth, water, air, and fire – mixed in various proportions. In the next century Aristotle thought there might be a fifth element – the ether. Leucippus (5th century BC) had another theory that there was just one kind of matter. He thought that if matter was repeatedly cut up, the end result would be an uncuttable piece of matter. His follower Democritus (about 400 BC) called these indivisible pieces of matter "atoms" (pp. 34-35), meaning "uncuttable." But Aristotle, who did not believe in atoms, was the most influential philosopher for the next 2,000 years, and his ideas about elements prevailed.

THE FOUR ELEMENTS IN A LOG
Empedocles's idea of the four elements was linked to certain properties. Earth was dry and cold, water was wet and cold, fire was hot and dry, and air was hot and wet. In the burning log below, all four elements can be seen. Empedocles thought that when one substance changes into another – such as when a burning log gives off smoke, emits sap, and produces ash – the elements that make up the log are separating or recombining under the influence of two forces. These forces were love (the combining force), and hate or discord (the separating force).

Empedocles

Design on the coin has been smoothed away

WEARING SMOOTH
Ancient philosophers thought that when objects such as coins and statues wore smooth with the passing of time they were losing tiny, invisible particles of matter.

MODEL OF WATER
Plato (4th century BC) thought that water was made up of icosahedrons, a solid shape with 20 triangular faces.

LIQUID FROM A LOG
Empedocles believed that all liquids, even thick ones like the sap that oozes from a burning log, were mainly water. His theory also held that small amounts of other elements would always be mixed with the main element.

Sap is made from the element water

ELEMENTAL ATOMS
Democritus developed the theory of atoms and combined it with the theory of elements. Like Plato, he thought there were only four shapes of atom, one for each element. He argued against the religious beliefs of his day, claiming that atoms moved randomly, and that there were no gods controlling the universe.

MODEL OF EARTH
Atoms of earth were thought by Plato to be cubes, which can stack tightly together to give strength and solidity.

ASHES TO ASHES
The theory of the elements suggested that ash and cinders were mainly made of the element earth, with a little of the element fire. At the end of the burning process, there was not enough fire left for more ash to be produced, but some fire remained for a while in the form of heat. The Greeks thought that the elements earth and water had a natural tendency to fall.

Ash and cinders are mainly the element earth

THE FIVE ELEMENTS
The human figure in this engraving is standing on two globes, representing earth and water, and is holding air and fire in his hands. The sun, moon, and stars are made of the ether, the fifth element.

MODEL OF AIR
Plato's model of an air atom was an octahedron, a solid figure with eight faces.

Smoke is mostly air, with some earth in the form of soot mixed in

NO SMOKE WITHOUT FIRE
When a piece of matter is burned, the element air inside was thought to be released in the form of smoke. The Greeks thought that air, like fire, had a natural tendency to rise.

MODEL OF FIRE
According to Plato, the atom of fire was a solid shape with four sides called a tetrahedron.

PENETRATING FLAMES
The element fire could be seen most clearly in flames and sparks, but the Greeks thought that some fire was present in everything. Plato's model of the fire atom is sharp and pointed. This is because heat seemed to be able to penetrate virtually every piece of matter.

Flames and sparks are the element fire

Investigating matter

Ideas about matter and how it behaved changed little for hundreds of years. But in Europe during the 16th and 17th centuries "natural philosophers" looked again at the ancient theories about matter. They tested them, together with newer ideas about how matter behaved, by experiments and investigations, and used the newly invented microscope and telescope to look closely at matter. Measurements became more precise. News of discoveries was spread by the printing press. The scientific revolution had begun.

Flow of sand is regulated by the narrow glass channel

SANDS OF TIME
The sandglass was a simple timing device, which allowed scientists to work out how fast objects fell, or how long it took for chemicals to react. More accurate measurements of time were not possible until after the first pendulum clock was made in 1657.

LABORING IN THE LAB
This 17th-century laboratory illustrates just some of the processes used by "natural philosophers" to find out about matter.

Eyepiece

HEATING AND COOLING MATTER
Very early experiments showed the effects of heating or cooling of matter. Philo of Byzantium constructed his lead thermoscope (Greek for "observing heat") about 250 BC. When the globe on the right is warmed, the air inside expands and pushes its way up the tube, which is immersed in the water on the left. If the heat is strong enough, bubbles of air escape. When the globe is cooled, the air contracts and water is drawn back up the tube.

Tiny bubbles of air

Reconstruction of Philo's thermoscope

Lead globe is full of air

Object to be viewed is placed on the glass

Glass globe contains water

Engraved scale

MARKINGS FOR MEASURING
Scientific investigations often involved measuring the exact amount of a liquid. This tall measuring cylinder has a scale of accurate markings for this purpose, while the specific gravity bottle has just one very accurate marking. When the liquid inside is weighed, its density can be calculated.

Single accurate marking

Small lens focuses light

Tilting mirror

SMALL WONDER
Microscopes began to open up the world of the very small from the mid-1500s onward. In the mid-1600s Anton van Leeuwenhoek found that a single drop of pond water could contain 8 million "animalcules" – tiny but intricately constructed creatures and plants. The more elaborate microscope shown here was made by Edmund Culpeper of London, in about 1728. It used a tilting mirror, visible at the bottom, to reflect light onto a specimen mounted above it on glass.

Enlarged view of a deathwatch beetle

DEGREES OF ACCURACY
As scientists looked closer at matter, they needed ever more accurate ways of measuring what they saw. This thermometer, a device for measuring changes in temperature, was made in Florence, Italy, in the 18th century. The bulb at the bottom contained alcohol, which expanded when it became warmer and moved along the coiled tube. The tube is marked with dots at equal intervals.

Dots are regularly spaced

Bulb of alcohol

NOVA
ATLANTIS
PER
FRANCISCUM BACONUM,
Baronem de Verulamio,
Vice-Comitem S. Albani.

VLTRAIECTI.
Apud Ioannem à VVuesberge,
Anno clɔ lɔ cXLIII.

SCIENTIFIC IMPROVEMENTS
Francis Bacon (1561-1626), the English philosopher, hoped that the new science could increase human well-being. *The New Atlantis* was his 1626 account of an imaginary society, or "utopia," where the government organized teams of scientists to conduct research and use the results to improve industry.

Ivory arm

Brass ring

Pointer indicates equilibrium

Cord fulcrums

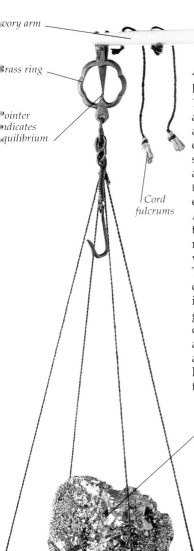

Alchemy

Before the scientific revolution of the 17th century, the closest approach to a systematic study of matter was alchemy – the "science" of changing one substance into another. This was studied in Egypt, China, and India at least as early as the 2nd century BC, and from the Middle East it eventually reached Europe. Alchemists learned much from the practical skills of dyers and metalworkers, and borrowed various ideas from astrologers. They tried, without success, to change "base" metals, such as lead, into precious ones, such as silver or gold. This series of operations was described as "killing" the metal and then "reviving" it. Alchemists also attempted to make the elixir of life, a potion that would give them the secret of everlasting life.

QUEST FOR GOLD
Alchemists used all kinds of scientific instruments and chemical processes in their mystical quest for gold. The laboratory above was imagined by a 19th-century painter.

Spoutlike alembic sits on the cucurbit

Alembic and cucurbit

PURE MATTER
Cucurbits and alembics were used by many alchemists to purify liquids. As the cucurbit was heated, vapor from the liquid inside rose to the top, then cooled and condensed. The pure liquid dripped from the alembic and was then collected.

"Fool's gold" – a compound made up of iron and sulfur

HANGING IN THE BALANCE
Scales are one of the most basic of measuring instruments. The weight at the right of these Chinese scales is moved along the longer arm until it balances the object in the pan. This particular method is quick, convenient, and fairly accurate. It was not until the 17th century that chemists realized that accurately weighing the substances involved in a chemical reaction is crucial to understanding what is going on.

Compound counterbalance

Greek lead weight

Solid matter

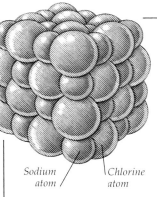

Sodium atom / Chlorine atom

HELD IN PLACE
As in most solids, the atoms (pp. 34-35) in this model of salt hold each other firmly in place, and form a regular pattern.

EVER SINCE PEOPLE began to observe the world carefully, they have classified matter into three main states – solids, liquids (pp. 18-19), and gases (pp. 20-21). A piece of solid matter has a fairly definite shape, unlike a liquid or a gas. Changing the shape of a solid always requires a certain amount of force, which can be either large or small. Squeezing or stretching a solid can change its volume (the amount of space it takes up) but generally not by very much. When they are heated, most solids will turn to liquid, then to gas as they reach higher temperatures. However, some solids such as limestone (pp. 36-37) decompose when they are heated. Crystals (pp. 14-15) and metals (pp. 16-17) are two of the most important kinds of solid.

Screw

Gimbal ring keeps the compass level even when the ship is rolling

SOLID STRENGTH
Brass, which is a combination of metals, or an alloy (pp. 16-17), is made of copper and zinc. It is used for the compass's gimbal ring, mounting ring, and pivot. Brass is strong, so the gimbal ring's mountings will not quickly wear out. Like many metals, brass is not magnetic, and will not interfere with the working of the compass needle.

SOLID PROPERTIES
Like most artificial objects, this 19th-century mariner's compass contains several kinds of solids. The compass has been taken apart on these two pages to reveal four solids – metal, cardboard, wood, and glass. All the solids in the compass have been chosen for their special and varied properties.

Mariner's compass in its protective wooden box

Mounting ring fixes the compass in its case and holds it under the glass

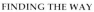

Magnet

Pins are attracted to the ends of the magnet

MAKING MAGNETS
The ancient Chinese are thought to be the first magnet makers. They discovered that iron can be magnetized by making it red-hot and then letting it cool while aligned in a north-south direction.

Hole which rests on pointed pivot

FINDING THE WAY
Beneath the compass card is a magnet, made either of iron or a rock called a lodestone. Magnets attract or repel each other, and also respond to the earth's magnetic poles. They tend to swing into a north-south line if they are free to move. The compass showed the mariner the angle between the direction of the ship and the north-south direction of the magnet.

SIZE AND STRENGTH
Galileo Galilei (1564-1642) studied materials' strength and showed that there is a limit to land animals' size. If the largest dinosaur had doubled in size, its bones would have become larger and stronger. However, the increase in the dinosaur's weight would have been even greater, making its bones snap.

AT FULL STRETCH
Many solids are elastic – after being stretched or squeezed, they return to their original shape. A rubber band, for example, can be stretched to more than double its length and then return to its original length. But if a material is distorted too much its shape may be permanently altered.

Pointed pivot supports the compass

Brass knobs sit in holes in the gimbal ring

Glass flows over hundreds of years

QUALITIES OF WOOD
The protective container of the compass needs to be strong, and to be rigid (keep its shape). Wood has many different qualities – the wood used for this container is fairly hard and long-lasting. Yet it is also soft and light enough to be easily worked with metal tools, and can be carved to form a smooth bowl shape.

SEEING THROUGH THINGS
The top of the compass needs to be transparent and strong. It is made of glass – halfway between a solid and a liquid (pp. 24-25). Glass may seem rigid, but over hundreds of years it gradually flows and becomes distorted. Most solids block light completely, but the clearest kinds of glass absorb little of the light passing through them.

DIFFERENT VIEWS
Transparent (see-through) materials can give a clear and undistorted view, as in the glass front of a watch. Or they can be deliberately shaped to help give an even clearer view, as in eyeglasses.

Diamond
10

Considerable difference in hardness between diamond and the other minerals on the scale

FROM SOFT TO HARD
Scientists classify solid materials by their hardness, on a scale from one to ten named after Friedrich Mohs (1773-1839). These solids are all minerals (so-called because they are usually mined). Talc is the softest at one, and diamond the hardest at ten. Any solid on the scale will scratch a softer one, and will itself be scratched by a harder one.

Compass direction points

PAPER POINTERS
The compass points are printed on paper or cardboard. Paper is made by pulping up wood and treating it to make it soft and flexible. It consists of countless fibers, and absorbs ink well because the ink lies in the spaces between the fibers.

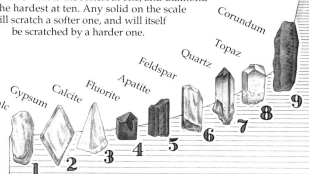

Corundum

Topaz

Quartz

Feldspar

Apatite

Fluorite

Calcite

Gypsum

Talc

1 2 3 4 5 6 7 8 9

The world of crystals

Crystals have been viewed with awe since ancient times. They are often very beautiful, and their shapes can differ widely, yet all crystal forms are of just six basic kinds. The orderly shape of each crystal is created by the arrangement of the atoms (pp. 34-35) inside. With the help of powerful microscopes, many objects and materials that seem irregularly shaped to the naked eye, such as stalactites and most metals, can be seen to be masses of tiny uniform crystals. Many crystals are valuable in industry, and some, such as quartz (used in watches) and silicon (used in computers), can be made in the laboratory.

SIX SHAPES
Abbé René Haüy (1743-1822) was one of the first to show that crystal shapes fall into six geometrical groups. He suggested how they could be built up by stacking identical units in regular patterns.

SCULPTED WATER
Stalactites are mainly limestone, created by centuries of dripping water. The atoms in the limestone have arranged themselves in regular crystalline patterns.

Identical cubes

CRYSTAL CUBES
Wooden models like this octahedron (eight-faced solid) were used by Abbé Haüy to explain how crystal forms arise. The cube-shaped units of this crystal model are arranged in square layers, each larger than the previous one by an extra "border" of cubes.

Tourmaline forms fine, long crystals with a cross-section that is triangular with rounded corners

HIGH-RISE CRYSTALS
Tourmaline crystals up to 10 ft (3 m) long have been found. They can occur in a wide variety of colors and are prized as gems. If warmed, one end of a tourmaline crystal becomes positively charged, and the other end becomes negatively charged.

THE EMERALD CITY
Crystals are often used as symbols of perfection and power. The magical Emerald City appears in the 1939 film *The Wizard of Oz*.

Outer part of the bismuth cooled fast and formed only microscopic crystals

Yellow sulfur crystals

Needle-shaped crystals formed where alloy solidified slowly

Crystals formed where the metal solidified slowly

BOXLIKE BISMUTH
Inside this piece of bismuth are intricate "nests" of crystal boxes, formed as the metal slowly solidified.

MELLOW YELLOW
At low temperatures, fairly flat sulfur crystals form. At high temperatures they are needle-shaped.

METAL MIXTURE
The thin, pointed crystals shown here are alloys (pp. 16-17) of copper and aluminum.

Outer part of alloy cooled fast and formed few crystals

Aragonite often forms
twin crystals

AMAZING ARAGONITE
Crystals of aragonite can be found in
limestone caves and hot springs. They take
many forms, such as fibers, columns, or
needles. Their color is usually white,
yellow, green, or blue.

MAKING CRYSTALS CLEAR
William Hyde Wollaston (1766-1828) made
important contributions to crystallography (the
scientific study of crystals). He recognized that a
cubic crystal, for example, did not have to be
built from cubes. Instead, it could be assembled
from atoms of other shapes, as in his wooden
models shown on this page. Scientists now know
that atoms can take very complicated shapes
when they join together.

EGG-SHAPED ATOMS
In this model made by Wollaston, the
atoms in the crystal are imagined to be egg-
shaped. Each has six neighbors at the
sides, forming a strong
horizontal layer.

LOOSE LAYERS
If atoms in crystals are
spheres, Wollaston
realized that they would
have neighbors on all
sides. They would not
form such strong layers
as the atoms of the other
shapes shown here.

FLAT ATOMS
Wollaston thought that if crystal atoms
are flat, they would link most strongly
where their flat faces were in contact.
They might form columns or fibers.

Azurite
crystals are
"knobbly"

BLUE IS THE COLOR
The mineral azurite is blue, as its name implies. In
the past azurite was crushed and used as a pigment.
It contains copper and is found with deposits of
copper ore. When azurite is made into a gem, it can
be faceted – cut to display polished flat faces.

LINING UP LIQUID CRYSTALS
Some crystals are liquid. The
particles in a liquid can be
temporarily lined up in regular
arrays when an electric or magnetic
field is applied. The liquid crystals
shown here were revealed under
an electron microscope. The liquid
affects light differently when the
crystals form, and can change from
being transparent to being opaque,
or colored. In digital clocks and
watches, calculators, or laptop
computers, electricity is used to
alter segments of the display from
clear to dark, to generate the
changing numbers or letters.

Metals and alloys

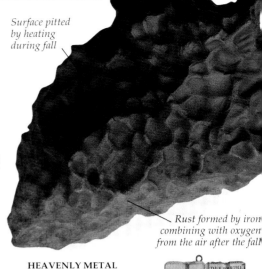

Surface pitted by heating during fall

THE THREE METALS most widely used are iron, steel, and aluminum. Iron and aluminum are both metallic elements (pp. 32-33), but steel is a mixture of iron and carbon. Such a combination, either of metals, or of metals and non-metals, is called an alloy. Combining a metal with other substances (either metallic or non-metallic) usually makes it stronger. Most metals are found in ore (rock), combined with other elements such as oxygen and sulfur. Heating the ore separates and purifies the metal. When metals are pure they are shiny, can be beaten into shape, and drawn out into wires. They are not brittle, but are often rather soft. Metals are good conductors (carriers) of electric current and heat.

Rust formed by iron combining with oxygen from the air after the fall

GOLDEN CHARACTER
Gold is a precious metal. It is rare and does not tarnish. It can be beaten into sheets of gold leaf, which are used to decorate letters in illuminated manuscripts like the one above.

HEAVENLY METAL
A very pure iron comes from certain meteorites. They are bodies that have fallen to Earth from outer space and have been partly burned away by the friction of entering the Earth's atmosphere.

Mercury expands along thin tube when heated

CUTTING EDGE
The use of bronze dates from about 5000 BC in the Middle East, and 2000 BC in Europe. Bronze is an alloy of copper and tin. It is very hard, and was used for the blades of axes, daggers, swords, and razors.

Blade of hammered bronze

Ancient Egyptian razor

Bulb contains mercury

HARD WORDS
Aluminum makes up one-twelfth of the rock near the Earth's surface. It was discovered in 1809, but only came into widespread use after 1886. It is a very light metal, and was first used in jewelery and novelties, like this picture postcard. Aircraft parts are often made of aluminum alloys.

LIQUID METAL
The metal mercury, sometimes known as quicksilver, is a liquid at normal temperatures. It expands by a relatively large amount when warmed, and has long been used in instruments to measure temperature, such as this 18th-century thermometer.

Bronze handle

Molten pig-iron poured in

Henry Bessemer

Converter

Air blown through inlets and carbon burned off

Purified iron poured into ladle

MAN OF STEEL
Henry Bessemer (1813-1898) greatly speeded up the steel-making process in the mid-19th century with his famous converter. Air was blown through molten pig iron (iron ore that had been heated in a furnace with coal or wood). This burned off the carbon (pp. 40-41) from the coal or wood in a fountain of sparks. The purified iron, still molten, was tipped out of the converter, and measured amounts of carbon and metals, such as nickel, manganese, or chromium, were added. These other substances turned the molten iron into steel, an alloy that is renowned for its strength.

BELL OF BRONZE

Metals such as bronze are ideal for bells because they vibrate for a long time after being struck. From about 1000 BC bronze has been cast (poured in a molten state into a mold). Once cast, large bells must cool very slowly to prevent cracking. The Liberty Bell, which hangs in Philadelphia, Pennsylvania, weighs about 2,079 lb (943 kg), and is about 3 ft (1 meter) high. It was made in London and delivered in 1752, but it cracked and had to be recast twice before it was hung. It cracked again in 1835 and in 1846. Since then it has never been rung.

PURE QUALITY

Goldsmiths formerly judged gold's purity by scraping it on a type of dark rock called touchstone. Its streak was then compared with the streaks made by the gold samples on two "stars." The best match came from gold of the same purity.

Sample has 875 parts of gold per thousand

Sample has 125 parts of gold per thousand

Streaks left by scraping samples on touchstone

Steel spring

Steel wheels

MULTIPURPOSE METALS

Various metals, each with its own particular job to do, are used in this old clock. The springs, chain, and cogwheels inside, which receive the most wear, are made of steel. The case is made of brass, an alloy of copper and zinc that is not so strong as steel. To make it look attractive, the brass has been gilded (coated with gold).

Cross-section of transatlantic cable

Rubberlike gutta-percha prevents electricity from leaking

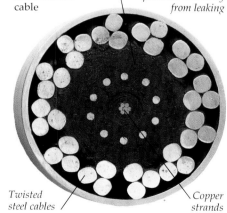

DEEP COMMUNICATION

A telegraph cable 2,325 miles (3,740 km) long was first laid across the seabed of the Atlantic Ocean in 1850, linking Britain with the US. The outer part of a typical cable was a strong sheath of twisted steel cables. It would resist rusting even in seawater (a solution known to rust metals quickly).

Twisted steel cables

Twisted steel cables

Copper strands

OCEAN CURRENT

A seven-stranded copper wire lies at the heart of the undersea cable. Copper was chosen for the wire because of its very useful properties. It is an excellent carrier of electric current and is easily drawn out into wires.

Properties of liquids

ACCORDING TO THE GREEKS who believed in the four elements, all liquids contain a large proportion of water (pp. 8-9). However, those who believed in atoms (pp. 34-35) thought that the atoms in a liquid could slide around one another, making the liquid flow to take the shape of its container. This is also the modern view. Liquid particles attract each other and keep close together, so they cannot be easily squeezed into a smaller volume or stretched out into a larger one. When a liquid is heated, however, the spacing between the particles generally increases in size, so the liquid expands. When a liquid is cooled, the reverse effect occurs, and the liquid contracts. It is possible for liquids to dissolve some solid substances. For example, salt placed in water seems to disappear very slowly. In fact the salt breaks up into individual atoms of sodium and chlorine (pp. 50–51). The ions spread out through the water, forming a mixture (pp. 26-27) called a solution of salt in water. Liquids can also dissolve gases and other liquids.

Hydrogen atom

Oxygen atom

SLIPPING AND SLIDING
The smallest unit of water consists of one atom (pp. 34-35) of oxygen joined to two hydrogen atoms. These clusters of three atoms slide around each other in liquid water.

PRESSING MATTER
Most liquids, particularly water and oil, act as good transmitters of pressure. In 1795 Joseph Bramah (1749-1814) patented his hydraulic press, in which compressed fluid multiplied the force that could be exerted by a human operator.

SLOW FLOW
Some liquids flow easily, but honey flows very slowly, and is described as being "viscous." Liquids such as tar and pitch (a substance used to seal roofs) are even more viscous.

Slow-moving liquid

Droplets are forced into shape by surface tension

Meniscus

Level surface

Gas in a liquid is pressed into spherical or almost spherical bubble shapes by the surrounding liquid

Liquid spreads out in a thin film

CURVED EDGE
The surface of an undisturbed liquid is horizontal, except at the very edge, where it forms a curve called a meniscus. The meniscus can be sloped up as it is here, or sloped down.

UPLIFTING MATERIAL
Because a liquid can flow, an object can be pushed down into it, forcing some of the liquid aside. But the displaced liquid tries to flow back, pushing the object upward. The object then seems lighter than the liquid, and floats, like this boat.

Narrow neck of vessel causes liquid to speed up as it flows through

WORN DOWN BY WATER
Given sufficient time, flowing liquids wear away solid surfaces, even rocks. The abrasive effect is increased when the liquid carries solid particles of rock and mud. Some rocks, such as clays and sandstones, have a low resistance to erosion. This canyon in the Arizona desert has been worn away by 10,000 years of flash floods.

Fast-moving liquid

Liquid takes the shape of its container

THE STRENGTH OF MOVING LIQUIDS
A stream of liquid can deliver a powerful force – a tsunami, or "tidal wave," can sweep away towns. Slower-moving liquid has time to break up and flow round obstacles, and does them less damage. Where a liquid has escaped from a container, surface tension (the inward pull at the surface) tries to pull it into shape. But because it is a relatively weak force, surface tension can pull only small amounts into drops – larger quantities of liquid are chaotic and formless.

WATER POWER
Streams and rivers have been used to turn waterwheels since ancient times. In 18th-century Britain water-powered looms featured heavily in the Industrial Revolution. Today, water from lakes, reservoirs, or the sea is used to turn electricity-generating turbines worldwide.

Level surface

BRIMMING OVER
The tiny particles that make up a liquid are held together by their attraction to each other. Surface tension makes the surface of a liquid behave like the tight elastic skin of a balloon. The wine in this glass is above the brim, but surface tension stops it from overflowing.

WALKING ON WATER
Surface tension lets this insect's feet walk instead of swim; its feet make dents in the water but don't go through.

Gases and their properties

ANCIENT PHILOSOPHERS WERE PUZZLED by the exact nature of gases. They realized air was not empty space. Some guessed the smell of a perfume was due to the spreading of tiny particles, and that frost was formed by the condensation of invisible water vapor. Many observed that the wind bent trees and vigorous bubbling made water froth. These early philosophers believed there was a single element of air (pp. 8-9), which had "levity," a tendency to rise. In the 17th century Evangelista Torricelli (1608-1647) showed that air, like solids and liquids, can be weighed. In the next century, chemists showed that air is a mixture of gases, and identified the gases given off in chemical reactions. These newly discovered gases were soon put to use; for instance, gas obtained from coal produced light and heat.

Carbon atom

Oxygen atom

IT'S A GAS
Gases, like the carbon dioxide shown here, consist of molecules (pp. 36-37) that are separated from each other, and which are constantly moving. Gas molecules are usually complex, made up of atoms (pp. 34-35) that are closely bound together.

Glass dome is emptied of air when the pump operates

Bung

Oxygen travels down the tube

Heating the potassium permanganate crystals gives off oxygen

Piston

Cylinder

Handle

Tube connecting cylinders to glass dome

AIRLESS EXPERIMENTS
The airpump shown here was built by Francis Hauksbee (1666-1713). The lever was worked to operate twin pistons, which removed air from the glass dome. Experiments could then be performed under the dome in an airless environment. The first airpump was made in the 1650s by Otto von Guericke (1602-1686), to demonstrate the strength of air pressure.

LIBERATING OXYGEN
When a solid is heated, it can often give off a gas. The crystals of potassium permanganate are composed of potassium, manganese, and oxygen. When heated, the crystals break down into other substances, and give off oxygen gas. The oxygen occupies a much larger volume as a gas than when it was combined in the solid, and escapes from the end of the tube. The gas is less dense than water, and bubbles to the top of the collecting jar.

Test tube stand

Bunsen burner

Gas supply

PRESSING FORCE

A barometer measures changes in atmospheric pressure. The early barometer made by Evangelista Torricelli had a mercury-filled upright glass tube. The tube's open end dipped in a bowl of mercury. Atmospheric pressure forced the mercury down in the bowl, and balanced the weight of the mercury in the tube.

A VALUABLE COLLECTION
This apparatus was used by Joseph Priestley (1733-1804) to collect gases. The gases would bubble up through the water and be collected for experimentation in the glass jars.

HIGH ACHIEVER

Jacques Charles (1746-1823) discovered an important law about the expansion of gases when heated (p. 39). In 1783 he took part in the first flight in a hydrogen balloon. Hydrogen is very light and also highly flammable, but was still being used in airships in the 1930s.

GAS WORKER

In 1775 Joseph Priestley discovered oxygen during his work with mercuric oxide. He found that oxygen supported breathing and burning, but did not recognize its exact nature. Using carbon dioxide from a local brewer to make water fizzy, he invented soda water.

Gas jar

Gas pressure pushes water out of the gas jar into the trough

Oxygen bubbles become larger as they reach the surface

"Beehive" stand for jar

Water

ENERGY FROM SUNLIGHT

Photosynthesis is the process by which green plants take energy from sunlight, and produce food molecules from carbon dioxide and water. Parts of this process can be seen here, when sunlight shines on freshly cut leaves immersed in water. The oxygen from the carbon dioxide molecules is released, and is given off into the water in the form of small bubbles. They rise to the surface and push water out from the jar.

Trough

Water pushed out from the jar

Gas pressure pushes water out from the jar

Oxygen bubbles

Changes of state

MATTER CAN BE ALTERED in various ways. Heating a solid to a temperature called its melting point will make it change state – it will turn into a liquid. Heating a liquid to a temperature called its boiling point has a similar effect – the liquid will change state and turn into a gas. It is possible to affect both the melting and the boiling point of matter. For example, if an impurity such as salt is added to ice, the melting point of the ice is lowered. The mixture (pp. 26-27) of salt and ice will melt, while pure ice at the same temperature will remain frozen. If salt is added to water, it raises the boiling point, and the water boils at a higher temperature. Pressure can also affect the state of matter. Where air pressure is low, the boiling point of water is lowered. An increase in pressure will lower the melting point of a solid.

YIELDING TO PRESSURE
Where a wire presses on ice, the melting point is lowered, and the ice melts. The wire cuts through the ice, which freezes again as the wire passes.

FROM SOLID TO GAS
In the following sequence, heating a solid – ice – to its melting point makes it change state to a liquid. Heating the liquid – water – to its boiling point makes it change state to a gas.

DROPPING LEAD
Bullets and lead shot used to be made by letting drops of molten lead fall from the top of a "shot tower." While still liquid, the lead droplets formed spheres, and then "froze" in this shape.

A WEALTH OF SUBJECTS
Scientist John Tyndall (1820-1893) was very interested in how heat causes changes of state. He also studied many other subjects, including the origins of life, and why the sky is blue.

1 SOLID STATE
Like most other substances, water can exist as a solid, liquid, or gas. The solid state is ice, and it forms when liquid water is cooled sufficiently. Ice may look different from water, but chemically it is exactly the same.

Pump to remove air from large flask

Stopcocks open to let air flow from small flask to large one

REDUCING THE PRESSURE
Tyndall's apparatus, shown here, demonstrates that water that is not hot enough to boil at ordinary atmospheric pressure will begin to boil when the pressure on it is reduced.

Water is placed inside this flask

Bunsen burner, the heat source

Almost all air is removed from this flask

Each piece of ice has a definite shape

PRESSURE AT WORK
This is a cast-aluminum pressure cooker from about 1930. The very high pressure in a pressure cooker allows water to be heated above its normal boiling point, and the food inside is quickly cooked.

Safety valve

Pressure gauge

Holes formed by bubbles of gas

STONE FROM A VOLCANO
Pumice stone is molten lava which has cooled very quickly. It is honeycombed with holes, which are "frozen-in" bubbles of gas.

MOLTEN MOUNTAIN
When a volcano erupts, it can violently expel thousands of tons of lava – red-hot molten rock from the Earth's core. As the lava cools it changes state and solidifies.

HIDDEN HEAT
Joseph Black (1728-1798) measured the heat needed to turn a solid into a liquid, or a liquid into a gas. He called this heat "latent," or hidden.

2 LIQUID STATE
When ice is warmed, it can turn into liquid water. This change happens at a definite temperature, which is normally 32° F (0° C). Under normal pressure water stays liquid up to 212° F (100° C).

3 GAS STATE
When water is heated sufficiently, it starts to turn into steam – a colorless, invisible gas. It can be "seen" only as bubbles in water. What is usually called steam is really a fine mist of water droplets.

Gas turns into liquid water where it touches a cooler surface

Bubbles of steam form in the liquid

Steam is invisible

A liquid's surface is horizontal

A liquid takes the shape of its container

Colloids and glasses

Some matter is difficult to classify. For example, lead, a metal, flows like a liquid over centuries. Glass, a seemingly solid substance, is actually a supercool liquid, and flows over decades. The atoms (pp. 34-35) in such substances are not firmly locked into a regular pattern. Instead they form a disorderly pattern, and the atoms move around, allowing the substance to flow. In a form of matter called a colloid, one substance is dispersed through another. The dispersed particles are much larger than atoms, but too small to be seen by the naked eye. Colloids include colored glass (solid particles dispersed in a solid), clay (solid in liquid), smoke (solid in gas), milk (liquid in liquid), mist (liquid in gas), and foam (gas in liquid).

NATURAL GLASS
Obsidian forms from molten volcanic rock. The rock cools quickly, and the atoms cannot form a regular pattern. Ancient peoples used obsidian for arrowheads like the one above.

Carved obsidian makes a sharp arrowhead

Molten glass

Measuring mold

Strong shears

GLASSBLOWING
Glass is made by melting sand mixed with other ingredients, and then cooling the liquid rapidly. It was first made around 4000 BC in the Middle East. Glass was blown to fit tightly inside a mold from the 1st century AD. Most glassblowing is now done mechanically, but a traditional method is shown in the following sequence. It is now practiced only for specialized objects.

Soda ash (sodium carbonate)

Sand (silica)

Limestone (calcium carbonate)

Iron oxide gives a green color

Barium carbonate gives a brown color

1 A GLASS RECIPE
The main ingredient in the recipe for glass, called the batch, is sand. The next main ingredient is usually soda ash (sodium carbonate), which makes a glass that is fairly easy to melt. Limestone may be used to produce a water-resistant glass.

2 CUTTING GLASS
A large quantity of the molten glass is gathered on the end of an iron rod by the glassmaker. It is allowed to fall into a measuring mold, and the correct quantity is cut off, using a pair of shears. There are several other traditional glassmaking techniques. Flat glass for windows can be produced by spinning a hot molten blob of glass on the end of a rod. It is spread into a large disc, from which flat pieces can be cut. Glass with a decorated surface can be made by pressing molten glass into a mold.

A GOOD TURN
This 18th-century glassmaker is remelting and turning the rim of a glass before correcting its shape. Glass gradually becomes softer over a range of temperatures. In its semi-solid state, glass can easily be shaped into the desired form.

GAFFER AND SERVITOR
The gaffer, or master glassmaker, is making a thin stem for a drinking-glass. He rolls the iron rod on the arms of his chair, to keep the glass symmetrical. The servitor, or assistant, draws out one end of the glass with a rod, while the gaffer shapes and cuts the stem.

Hollow blowing-iron

Shaping mold

Layer of steam cushions the glass

Parison

Flat plate

Final product shows no signs of the joint between the two halves of the mold

3 MAKING THE PARISON
The correct quantity of molten glass is picked up from the measuring mold on a hollow blowing-iron and is reheated in a furnace. The glassmaker blows a little air through the blowing-iron and taps the glass on a flat plate a few times to shape it. The glass is now approximately the size and shape of the finished product – in this case a bottle – and is called a parison. Behind the parison is the open shaping mold, which is bottle-shaped. The parison is now ready to be placed inside.

4 BLOWING, MOLDING, AND SPINNING
When the mold has been tightly closed, the glass is gently blown again. The glass expands and takes the shape of the inside of the mold. As well as blowing, the glassblower also spins the blowing-iron rapidly. This ensures that the final object does not show any signs of the joint between the two halves of the mold, or any other defects. The glass never comes in direct contact with the material of the mold. This is because the inside of the mold is wet and a layer of steam forms, cushioning the glass.

5 ONE BROWN BOTTLE
The shaping mold is opened to reveal the final product – a reproduction of a 17th-century bottle. This specialized object has to be broken away from the blowing-iron. The jagged mouth of the bottle has to be finished off by reheating it in a furnace and using shaping tools. Since the glass has cooled slightly, the rich brown color provided by the special ingredients in the batch is revealed. In the very early days of glass, it was always colored. The first clear glass was made in the 1st century BC.

Mixtures and compounds

When salt and sand are mixed together, the individual grains of both substances can still be seen. This loose combination of substances is called a mixture. The mixture of salt and sand is easy to separate – if it is given a gentle shake, the heavier grains of sand settle to the bottom. Mixing instant coffee and hot water produces a closer combination, called a solution. Yet this is still fairly easy to separate. If the solution is gently heated, pure water is given off in the form of water vapor, while solid coffee is left behind. The closest combinations of substances are chemical. When carbon (in the form of charcoal) burns, oxygen from the air combines with it to form the gases carbon dioxide and carbon monoxide. These gases are difficult to break down, and are called compounds.

COLORFUL REPORT
Mixtures of liquids or gases can be separated by chromatography. The blotting paper shown here has been dipped into an extract of flower petals. Some of the liquid is drawn up into the paper, but the components flow at different rates, and separate out into bands of colors.

WHEAT FROM CHAFF
Traditionally, wheat was threshed to loosen the edible grains from the chaff (the husks). The grains and chaff formed a mixture that could be separated by "winnowing." Grains were thrown into the air and the breeze blew away the lighter chaff, while the grain fell back.

GOLD IN THE PAN
Gold prospectors have "panned" for gold since the 19th century. They swill gravel from a streambed around a pan with a little water. Any gold nuggets present separate from the stones because of their high density.

FAR FROM ELEMENTARY
In *The Sceptical Chymist*, published in 1661, Robert Boyle (1627-1691) described elements (pp. 32-33) as substances that could not be broken down into anything simpler by chemical processes. He realized that there are numerous elements, not just four (pp. 8-9). Boyle was one of the first to distinguish clearly between mixtures and compounds.

Blotting paper

Fastest moving component

Mashed petals and mineral alcohol

ANALYZING COMPOUNDS

This condenser was invented by the German chemist Justus von Liebig (1803-1873) around 1830, for analyzing carbon-containing compounds. The compound was heated into a gas, and passed over copper oxide in the glass tube. Oxygen from the copper oxide combined with carbon and hydrogen in the gas, and formed carbon dioxide gas and water vapor. The potassium hydroxide in the glass spheres absorbed the carbon dioxide. The amount of carbon in the original compound could be calculated by the increase in weight in the spheres.

Charcoal is used as the heat source

REFLECTIVE THINKER

Justus von Liebig made many advances in the chemistry of "organic" substances. This originally meant substances made in living organisms, but now refers to most carbon-containing substances (pp. 40-43). His scientific feats included devising standard procedures for the chemical analysis of organic compounds, inventing a method of making mirrors by depositing a film of silver on glass, pioneering artificial fertilizers, and founding the first modern teaching laboratory in chemistry.

RUSTING AWAY

The compound rust is a red solid. It forms when iron, a grayish solid, combines with the gases oxygen and hydrogen. When iron is exposed to air, rust forms spontaneously, but the reaction is not easily reversed – the compound can only be broken down again by chemical means.

SALT OF THE EARTH

In the 19th century salt was shown to be a compound of two previously unknown substances – sodium, a silvery metal, and chlorine, a poisonous gas.

Sample experiences a strong force

Glass tube contains copper oxide

Potassium hydroxide in the glass spheres absorbs the carbon dioxide

Calcium chloride in this tube absorbs water, allowing the amount of hydrogen in the compound to be calculated

IN A WHIRL

Mixtures of liquids, or suspensions of solids in liquids naturally separate out over a period of time. This process can be speeded up by whirling the sample round in a centrifuge.

Handle is connected to the shaft by gears so the speed of rotation is increased

Measuring device

Metal holders for the test tubes

Test tube

Hand centrifuge in action

Hand centrifuge is operated by turning the handle

Components of the hand centrifuge

SALT OF THE SEA

These salt pans in India are shallow pits that are flooded with seawater (a mixture of salt and water). The water evaporates in the hot sunshine, but only pure water comes off as a vapor. The salt is left behind as a white solid.

Conservation of matter

MATTER COMBINES, separates, and alters in countless ways. During these changes, matter often seems to appear and disappear. Hard deposits of scale build up in a kettle. Water standing in a pot dries up. Plants grow, and their increase in weight is much greater than the weight of the water and food that they absorb. In all everyday circumstances matter is conserved – it is never destroyed or created. The scale found in the kettle built up from dissolved matter that was present in the water all the time. The water in the pot turned into unseen gases that mingled with the air. The increased bulk of the plants came from the invisible carbon dioxide gas in the air. Only in nuclear explosions, or in the sun and stars, or in other extreme situations, can matter be created or destroyed (pp. 62-63).

GREAT SURVIVOR
The original matter in a long-dead organism is dispersed and survives. A fossil is the last visible trace of an organism.

THE BALANCE OF LIFE
Lavoisier weighed people and animals over long periods of time to discover what happened to their air, food, and drink. He calculated the quantities of gases involved by examining the measured quantities of solids and liquids that they had consumed.

WEIGHTY MATTER
In the late 18th century the balance became the chemist's most important measuring instrument. Accurate weighing was the key to keeping track of all the matter involved in a reaction. It led to the abandonment of the phlogiston theory (pp. 30-31) – that when a material burns, a substance called phlogiston is always released.

A COUPLE OF CHEMISTS
Antoine Lavoisier (1743-1794) stated the principle of conservation of matter in 1789. This was not a new idea – matter had been assumed to be everlasting by many previous thinkers. Lavoisier, however, was the first to demonstrate this principle actively. His wide-ranging investigations were renowned for their rigor – he carried out experiments that were conducted in sealed vessels, and made accurate records of the many substances involved in chemical reactions. This work was extremely careful and laborious, but he was aided by another talented chemist and devoted coworker, his wife, Marie-Anne.

Glass dome traps gases

Fresh pear

WEIGHING THE EVIDENCE
Lavoisier's theory of the conservation of matter can be effectively demonstrated by comparing the weight of substances before and after an experiment. Here, a pear is placed under an airtight container and weighed. The pear is left for a few days and then weighed again. The two weights can be compared to discover whether the process of decay has involved any overall weight change.

Pointer indicates that the pans are perfectly balanced

Potassium permanganate dissolves and forms a solution

Water

NATURAL EROSION

The land is constantly worn away by wind, rain, and waves, yet this is balanced by the natural building up of new land forms elsewhere. No matter is lost or gained overall.

Potassium permanganate crystals

AN OBVIOUS SOLUTION

Solids left in water often dissolve. If the solids are colorless, such as salt, it is easy to believe they have disappeared completely. In fact they have just thoroughly mixed, and broken into minute particles, which have spread through the liquid. When the solid is colored, like this potassium permanganate, it is easier to believe that it still exists in the liquid. Weighing the solution confirms that it weighs the same as the original liquid and solid.

OUT WITH A BANG

When fireworks go off, gunpowder burns, as well as other chemicals, plus the cardboard and paper of the firework packaging. The burning products form gases and a small quantity of solids. Though widely scattered, the combined products weigh the same as the original.

Glass dome contains air and gases produced by rotting pear

ROTTEN RESULT

After a few days, rotting begins to take place, and some parts of the pear become brown and mushy. In the air under the glass dome there is now less oxygen, for some of it combines with the substances in the pear. There is more carbon dioxide, however, as well as other gases released by the fruit. Overall, the weight of the container plus its contents does not alter in the slightest degree. Early chemists did not realize that if the glass dome is lifted before weighing, air is likely to enter or escape, and therefore affect the weight of the container and its contents.

Condensation

Rotting pear

Scale pan

Burning matter

ONE OF THE FIRST great achievements of 18th-century science was the explanation of burning (also known as combustion). Georg Stahl (1660-1734) put forward the theory that an element, phlogiston, was given out in burning. His theory was wrong – it would mean that all substances would lose weight when they burn. Several chemists had already observed that some substances such as metals increase in weight during burning, and the theory of phlogiston was firmly denied by Antoine Lavoisier (pp. 28-29). He argued that air contains a gas that combines with a substance when it burns, and he named the gas oxygen. Sometimes substances can "burn" in gases other than oxygen. Some, such as ammonium dichromate, can change by themselves into other substances, producing flame, heat, and light.

FROM CRYSTALS TO ASH
In the following sequence, orange ammonium dichromate crystals produce flame, heat, and light, and turn into gray-green ash.

Orange crystals of ammonium dichromate

Low flames

Ash quickly forms

1 READY TO REACT Ammonium dichromate is a substance used in indoor fireworks. It consists of nitrogen, hydrogen, chromium, and oxygen.

2 VITAL SPARK When lit by a flame, the substance's atoms (pp. 34-35) form simpler substances, and produce heat and light.

Brass pivot

Burning-lens is angled to catch sunlight

Wooden stand

Melting ice in flask

THE HEAT OF THE MOMENT
Antoine Lavoisier was particularly interested in chemical reactions that required great heat. One problem in his scientific work was to obtain heat that was both intense and "clean," for often the reacting substances were contaminated by smoke and soot from the heat source (usually a flame). His solution was this giant mobile burning-glass, or convex lens, with which he enthralled the French populace in 1774.

FOCUS OF ACTIVITY
Heat brings about many changes in matter. It can cause different substances to react together, or it can make a reaction go faster. Here the heat is produced as sunlight is focused by a large convex lens to fall on to a flask containing ice. This causes the ice to melt – a physical rather than a chemical change. If sunlight is focused on to paper, the paper can smolder, and even burst into flame. This is a chemical change, and is an example of combustion.

Higher, stronger flames

3 BREAKDOWN
The substance is rapidly converted into chromium oxide, a compound of chromium and oxygen, and into nitrogen and water vapor, both invisible gases.

4 ASHEN ENDING
The orange crystals of ammonium dichromate have broken down, leaving a large pile of chromium oxide. The nitrogen and water vapor have escaped into the air.

Gray-green ash of chromium oxide

Air is blown through the mouthpiece

A CHEMIST'S BLOWPIPES
These 19th-century blowpipes enabled a chemist to direct a thin jet of air accurately on to substances being heated in a flame. This produced intense heat at one spot.

Air is forced through the thin metal tube

Controllable flame comes out of the top of the burner

Large surface area increases the amount of heat that can be delivered

BUNSEN'S BRAINCHILD
The gas burner, invented by German chemist Robert Bunsen (1811-1899) provides a hot, controllable flame, and is still used today.

VERSATILE VALVE
The secret of the Bunsen burner lies in the adjustable air valve at the base of the tube, which can be opened in varying degrees to alter the intensity of the flame.

A BETTER BURN
This elaborate version of the laboratory gas burner was made in 1874. It increased the amount of heat that could be delivered.

Gas supply comes through this pipe

Air valve

Enamelled iron

Bunsen burner from 1889

Bunsen burner made from flame resistant porcelain

Charting the elements

ELEMENTS ARE PURE SUBSTANCES – they do not contain anything else, and cannot be broken down into simpler substances. Many of the elements were discovered during the 18th and 19th centuries, particularly by using processes such as electrolysis and spectroscopy. In electrolysis, an electric current is passed through compounds to break them down (pp. 50-51). In spectroscopy, the light given out by hot substances is analyzed with a spectroscope (pp. 56-57) to show an element's characteristic pattern of colors. Dmitri Mendeleyev (1834-1907) brought order to the elements with his "periodic table," based on patterns in properties of elements such as their reactivity.

FLAME TEST
Here common salt (sodium chloride) burns yellow in a flame, revealing the presence of the element sodium.

A BATTERY OF DISCOVERIES
After learning of Alessandro Volta's invention of the electric battery in 1800, Humphry Davy (1778-1829) built his own. It was large, and had 250 metal plates. He used it for electrolysis, and prepared pure samples of new metals.

W. A. TAYLOR'S "STUDENT'S GUINEA SET" OF BLOWPIPE APPARATUS AND PURE CHEMICAL RE-AGENTS.

SPLITTING UP SALT
Humphry Davy discovered sodium by electrolyzing molten salt in this apparatus. Davy used electrolysis to obtain other metals with similar properties to sodium, such as barium, potassium, magnesium, calcium, and strontium. He then used potassium to extract another new element, boron.

Terminal linked to battery

BURNING QUESTION
This box of flame test equipment dates from the 19th century. It includes a blowpipe, tweezers, and different chemicals for testing. In a flame test, tiny quantities of a substance are held on a wire, which is put in to a flame. The color of the flame often indicates the substance's identity. For example, a flame is turned violet by potassium, and blue-green by copper. Flame tests require the hot flame of the Bunsen burner (p. 31).

ELECTRICAL BREAKDOWN

Common salt consists of sodium and chloride ions – positively charged sodium atoms, and negatively charged chlorine atoms (pp. 50-51). When salt is melted, the ions move around each other. If metal plates connected to a battery are placed in the molten salt, the positive plate attracts the chloride ions, and the negative plate attracts the sodium ions.

Sodium deposited

Negatively charged chloride ion

Chlorine released

Positively charged sodium ion

Negative terminal linked to battery

Positive terminal linked to battery

Liquid compound was placed in glass dish to be electrolyzed

GETTING THE GREEN LIGHT

In 1861 William Crookes (p. 48) discovered a new element, thallium, by spectroscopy. His many samples of thallium compounds are shown here, with one of his notebooks detailing the discovery. He could detect minute quantities of the new element because it emits a brilliant green light when in a hot flame.

The periodic table

The properties of the elements can be described and understood in terms of the periodic table. It shows more than 100 elements, arranged vertically into columns (called groups) and horizontally into rows (called periods). Properties change systematically going down each group and along each period, but elements in each group have generally similar properties. For example, group VIII contains the very unreactive "noble" gases such as argon (Ar), while group I contains very reactive metals such as sodium (Na).

PATTERN FINDER

Dmitri Mendeleyev's periodic table suggested corrections to previously accepted chemical data, and successfully predicted the existence of new elements. The Russian periodic table shown here is based on Mendeleyev's original of 1869.

33

The building blocks

As SCIENTISTS DISCOVERED more elements, they pondered over the ultimate nature of matter. The ancient idea of atoms (pp. 8-9) received a boost from English chemist John Dalton (1766-1844) in 1808. He proposed that each element has its own unique atom, and that each compound is formed by a certain combination of atoms. He showed that the weights of atoms relative to each other could be found by weighing the elements that combined in particular compounds. The comparative weight of an atom could be found, but not the actual weight – a given atom could only be said to be so many times heavier than, for example, one of hydrogen, the lightest atom.

ATMOSPHERIC ATOMS
John Dalton drew these diagrams in 1802. He was an enthusiastic meteorologist and knew that air consists of oxygen, water vapor, carbon dioxide, and nitrogen (top diagram). He developed his atomic theory while explaining why these gases remain mixed, rather than forming separate layers.

CLOSING IN ON ATOMS
Atoms make up the world in much the same way that the letters of the alphabet make up a book. Scientists need a close-up view to study atoms, just as readers have to peer closely at a page to study individual letters.

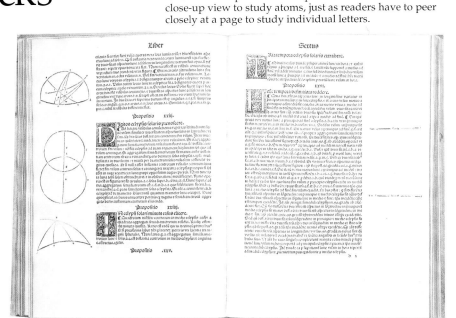

1 THE BOOK OF THE WORLD
A glance at any book shows that it is made up of many things, such as pictures, text of large and small print, and different chapters. Similarly, a glance at the "book of the world" shows that it is a kaleidoscopic array of many sorts of chemical substances. But such a glance does not reveal whether or not the world is made of atoms.

2 A PAGE AT A TIME
If a reader concentrates on one page of the "book of the world" and temporarily ignores the rest of the pages, this still gives a sample of the world that is very large compared with the atom. Similarly, when studying matter scientifically a small part must be isolated, for example, by examining a substance in a flask in a laboratory. To obtain a more detailed view of matter, scientists need to use instruments.

ELASTIC FLUIDS
Dalton assumed that gases are made of atoms which are far apart and can move independently. This is why gases can be compressed and expanded. He called gases "elastic fluids," and pictured their atoms like these circles.

Propofitio xxiiij.

N eclypfi folari minuta cafus elicere.
Quadratum diftatie centrozum in medio eclypfis aufer a
quadrato aggregati femidiametrozum refidui. Radix often/
dit minuta quefita. Ratio eft eade que in decimafeptima hui⁹
Et fi precifionis labo꞉ tibi placeret : poteris vti fcientia trian/
guli fpheralis. Nam latus.g.a.eft aggregatum femidiame/
trozum lune ꞇ folis.a.e.eft diftantia centrozum in medio eclypfis꞉ꞇ angulus
e.eft rectus.igitur.

John
Dalton

3 ENDLESS VARIETY
In close-up, one piece of text consists of many different words. Similarly, with the aid of chemical analysis and instruments, matter can be seen to be made up of an enormous number of different substances.

quadrato aggregati femidiametrozum refidui. Radix often/
dit minuta quefita. Ratio eft eade que in decimafeptima hui⁹
Et fi precifionis labo꞉ tibi placeret : poteris vti fcientia trian/
guli fpheralis. Nam latus.g.a.eft aggregatum femidiame/

4 NARROW VIEW
A microscope can give a detailed view of a small sample of matter, but this sample may be composed of a variety of substances. It is similar to a sentence, which is made up of many different words.

DALTON'S ATOMS AND ELEMENTS
In 1808 John Dalton published his atomic theory. It suggested that all matter is made up of indivisible atoms; each element is composed of atoms of characteristic weight; and compounds are formed when atoms of various elements combine in definite proportions. Below are Dalton's symbols for the atoms of the 36 elements that he believed to exist (over 100 elements have now been found). Some of Dalton's elements shown here, for example lime and soda, are actually compounds, not elements. Dalton also calculated the weight of each element's atom, by comparing it to hydrogen.

5 WORDS OF SUBSTANCE
"Words" in the "book of the world" are groups of atoms, or molecules (pp. 36-37). Here, the 26 letters of the Roman alphabet make up words. About 90 different kinds of atom make up molecules.

ELEMENTS

	wt			wt
Hydrogen	1	Strontian	46
Azote	5	Barytes	68
Carbon	54	Iron	50
Oxygen	7	Zinc	56
Phosphorus	9	Copper	56
Sulphur	13	Lead	90
Magnesia	20	Silver	190
Lime	24	Gold	190
Soda	28	Platina	190
Potash	42	Mercury	167

Dalton's elements

6 SINGULAR CHARACTERS
The letters on the printed page correspond to atoms. Just as letters group into words, so atoms form molecules. There is no limit to the words that can be formed from the alphabet, and any number of compounds can be formed from atoms. Not all possible combinations of letters are permitted, and neither are all combinations of atoms.

Dalton's carbon atom

Molecules

A<small>TOMS CAN EXIST SINGLY</small> in some gases, but in many substances they form groups called "molecules." For example, the molecule of water consists of an oxygen atom (O) joined to two hydrogen atoms (H). Its chemical formula is H_2O. Some molecules can be much bigger than this, containing thousands of atoms. In the mid-19th century it was realized that chemical bonds could explain the ways in which atoms link together to form molecules. A bond is like a hook that can link to a similar hook on another atom. For example, an atom of the gas nitrogen has three hooks, while a hydrogen atom has one. Each bond on the nitrogen atom can link to the bond on one hydrogen atom, which produces the molecule NH_3, the gas given off by smelling salts.

19th-century molecular model of monochloromethane, a type of solvent

Ammonia molecule (NH_3)

Chemical bond

Oxygen

Sulfur

Nitrogen

S

O

Hydrogen

Carbon

FITTING IT ALL TOGETHER
The carbon atom (C) has four bonds, nitrogen (N) three, hydrogen (H) one, and sulphur (S) and oxygen (O) each have two. Nitrogen combines with three hydrogens to form a molecule of ammonia (NH_3).

Calcium carbonate molecule ($CaCO_3$)

Carbon

O

C

O

Oxygen

Ca

Calcium

1 THE RAW MATERIAL
Limestone is a whitish rock with the chemical name of calcium carbonate. As this name suggests, the molecule of limestone contains atoms of calcium and carbon, but it also contains oxygen. Each atom of carbon is tightly joined to three of oxygen, and this group is more loosely linked to one atom of calcium.

Limestone breaks up when heated

Limestone (calcium carbonate)

Bunsen burner

Pestle Mortar Calcium hydroxide paste

FORCEFUL SUGGESTION
Jöns Jakob Berzelius (1779-1848) was one of the first people to suggest that atoms are held together in molecules by electrical forces (pp. 60-61).

ITALIAN IDEAS
Amedeo Avogadro (1776-1856) suggested that in equal volumes of any two gases there are always the same number of molecules, if the gases are at the same temperature and pressure. For about 50 years his idea was largely ignored, until another Italian chemist, Stanislao Cannizzaro (1826-1910), publicized it. The idea was then quickly accepted, and it helped to clarify many chemical reactions.

Water

Pipette

Crumbly powder (calcium oxide)

Hydrogen
Calcium
Oxygen
Calcium hydroxide molecule ($Ca(OH)_2$)

Oxygen
Carbon
Calcium
Calcium carbonate molecule ($CaCO_3$)

3 ADDING WATER
When water is added to calcium oxide powder there is a strong reaction, and the powder swells up and gives out heat. The molecules of the calcium oxide and of the water, H_2O, rearrange themselves to form molecules of calcium hydroxide, a soft and pasty substance. As its name suggests, this molecule contains calcium, hydrogen, and oxygen. Its formula is $Ca(OH)_2$, showing that two oxygen-hydrogen pairs (OH) are joined to a calcium atom.

4 BACK TO CALCIUM CARBONATE
The calcium hydroxide dries and hardens. Water molecules (H_2O) are given off into the air, while carbon dioxide molecules (CO_2) from the air are absorbed. The calcium hydroxide ($Ca(OH)_2$) turns into calcium carbonate ($CaCO_3$), chemically identical to the raw material. The reconstituted calcium carbonate looks different from the original limestone because it was not formed under high pressure within the Earth.

Carbon dioxide molecule (CO_2)
Carbon
Oxygen
Calcium
Calcium oxide molecule (CaO)

Tongs

2 HEATING THE LIMESTONE
When limestone is heated, it turns into a soft, crumbly powder called calcium oxide. This happens because each molecule of the original calcium carbonate breaks into two smaller molecules. One of these molecules consists of the calcium atom (Ca) joined to a single oxygen atom (O), making CaO. The other molecule consists of the carbon atom joined to the other two oxygen atoms, making CO_2. This is carbon dioxide gas, which escapes into the atmosphere.

Reconstituted calcium carbonate

Molecules in motion

Up until the mid-18th century, there was a widely accepted theory that heat was a "fluid" called caloric. However, in 1799 Count Benjamin Rumford (1753-1814) observed that limitless quantities of heat could be generated in the boring of cannon barrels. He suggested that the drilling work was increasing the motions of the atoms that made up the metal. This idea gained support when James Joule (1818-1889) did experiments to measure exactly how much work was needed to generate a definite amount of heat. When heat is applied to matter, the motion of the molecules is increased, and the temperature rises. Gradually it was realised that the differences between the three states of matter – solids, liquids, and gases (pp. 22-23) – are caused by the motion of molecules. The molecules in a solid are fixed, but can vibrate. The molecules in a liquid move around, but still remain in contact with each other. In a gas the molecules fly around freely, and move in straight lines until they collide with each other or with other objects.

Highly magnified pollen grains – the key to molecular movement

DANCE OF THE POLLEN
In 1827, Scotsman Robert Brown (1773-1858) observed pollen grains under a microscope. The grains were suspended in a liquid, and were in constant motion. He thought the motion originated in the pollen particles. But Albert Einstein (p. 55) in 1905, and Jean Perrin (1870-1942) in 1909, explained that the grains were being buffeted by the movement of the molecules in the liquid.

Pointer moves around the dial to show expansion of the rod

MEASURING HEAT EXPANSION
When a solid is heated, the vibration of its molecules increases. Each molecule then needs more space to vibrate, and the solid expands. This device, a pyrometer (meaning "heat-measurer") from the mid-19th century, showed how a metal rod increased in length as it was heated by a gas flame placed beneath it, and then shrank again as it cooled.

Lever turns when rod changes length

Alcohol burner for heating the rod

Metal rod to be heated

Clamp at fixed end of rod

Free end of rod moves as it expands

Support for free end of rod

Weight keeps lever mechanism in close contact with the end of the rod

*Handle to wind
up weight*

*String connected
to falling weight
turns rod*

TURNING TO HEAT
In the 1840s James Joule used this water friction apparatus to measure how much heat a given amount of mechanical "work" could be converted into. The work was done by a weight that turned paddles in a container of water. The fixed vanes limited the swirling of the water, so the work done was converted into heat. Joule measured the water's rise in temperature, and calculated the heat generated. His results added evidence to the theory that heat is the movement of molecules.

Paddles

TAKING TEMPERATURES
James Joule measured the "rate of exchange" between heat, mechanical work, and electrical energy.

RACING AHEAD
Ludwig Boltzmann (1844-1906) was one of the first scientists to assume that molecules in gases move at a range of speeds (previous scientists had assumed for simplicity that all molecules moved at the same speed). He calculated that gas molecules can rotate and vibrate, as well as move through space.

Water inlet

Water outlet

*Container insulates
apparatus from
outside heat*

*Fixed vanes resist
movement of water*

*Glass
separating
plate*

*Bromine
is brown*

UPWARDLY MOBILE
Gases expand to fill available space. Here, the gas bromine, which is heavier than air, is confined in the lower jar. But when the separating plate is removed, the bromine molecules diffuse into the upper jar.

*Molecules
exert
pressure as
they bounce
off walls of
container*

*External pressure
doubled*

BOYLE'S LAW
Robert Boyle (p. 26) saw that when a gas is pushed into a smaller volume, it exerts greater pressure. This is because the molecules hit the container walls more frequently.

Gas expands

*Gas
under
pressure*

CHARLES'S LAW
Jacques Charles (p. 21) saw that when a gas is heated, it exerts greater pressure, and will expand if it can. The molecules move faster and collide more violently with the container walls.

Carbon rings and chains

CLOSING THE CIRCLE
The structure of the benzene molecule, a form of carbon, resembles a snake swallowing its own tail.

CARBON IS UNIQUE in the number and complexity of compounds it can form. More than 7 million carbon-containing compounds are now known, compared with about 100,000 compounds made from all the other elements. Carbon is essential to the chemistry of all living things (pp. 42-43). The carbon atom can easily link up with other carbon atoms and with most other types of atom, using its four chemical "hooks," or valency bonds (pp. 36-37). Its molecules can have a "backbone" of a long chain of carbon atoms, either straight or branched. The carbon atoms can also form rings, which can be linked to other rings or carbon chains, to form intricate structures, sometimes consisting of thousands of atoms.

PREHISTORIC PRESSURE
Coal is the fossilized remains of trees and other plants that were buried in swamps. Over about 345 million years, they have been turned into a soft black rock by intense, sustained pressure from layers of other rocks. Coal consists mostly of carbon, with some hydrogen, oxygen, nitrogen, and sulfur. The carbon takes oxygen from the air and burns vigorously, so coal is a useful source of fuel.

Benzene

SMUDGY CARBON
Charcoal, a form of carbon, is obtained when substances such as wood, bone, or sugar are heated strongly with no air present. Charcoal is soft and easy to smudge, and is an excellent drawing material

Graphite

PLUMBING THE DEPTHS
Graphite, also known as plumbago, is a form of carbon found as a soft mineral. It can easily be made to split and flake. Graphite is the main component of pencil "leads," and is widely used as a lubricant

LORD OF THE RINGS
Friedrich Kekulé (1829-1896) tried for a long time to calculate how a benzene molecule's six carbon atoms link to the six hydrogen atoms. He found the solution while dozing. He dreamed of a row of carbon and hydrogen atoms closing in a ring, like a snake swallowing its tail.

Diamond molecule

Carbon atoms are arranged in an intricate lattice

Single bond

Diamonds

DIAMONDS ARE FOR EVER
The hardest natural material is diamond. It is a valuable gemstone, but is also used as the cutting tip in drills, or for grinding material. It consists of virtually pure carbon. Its atoms are arranged in a very strong three-dimensional lattice (a repeated pattern within a crystal). Each atom is joined to four neighbors by single chemical bonds. Diamonds form where carbon has been subjected to huge geological pressures and temperatures.

BAFFLING BENZENE
When coal is strongly heated, a colorless liquid – benzene – is obtained. The benzene structure is the basis of a huge number of important carbon compounds. Its molecular structure had baffled chemists until Kekulé thought of it as a ring of carbon atoms linked to hydrogen atoms.

Benzene molecule

Carbon atoms form a ring

Hydrogen atom

Single bond

Double bond

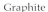

FAT FACTS
Butter is a mixture of fats – carbon-containing substances that are important in living things for storing energy. Similar substances that are liquid at room temperature are called oils.

Butter is an edible fat

Jet brooch

CLEANSING WITH CARBON
Soap is made from substances with long chains of carbon atoms, usually 15 or 17. One end of each soap molecule attaches to water and the other end attaches to oil. This enables soap to break up oil and grease into small drops in water.

BLACK BEAUTY
Jet is a form of coal called lignite, and is largely made up of carbon. It has a deep velvety black color, and is easy to carve and polish. Jet has been used for jewelery since early times.

Gasoline

Each cluster contains 60 carbon atoms

Octane molecule

Single bond

Carbon atom

Graphite molecule

Layer of carbon atoms

Hydrogen atom

Double bond

Single bond

ATOMS IN LAYERS
Graphite and diamond are the two crystalline forms of carbon. Unlike diamond, the carbon atoms in graphite are joined in flat layers. Each layer is only weakly joined to the next, and so the layered atoms can easily slip over each other.

GLOBULAR CARBON
One of the strangest forms of carbon to be discovered consists of globular clusters of carbon atoms. The computer graphics color representation shown here is the simplest form, with each globe containing 60 atoms. It is named buckminsterfullerene, after Buckminster Fuller (1895-1983), an inventor who developed the similarly shaped geodesic dome. Though only recently discovered, buckminsterfullerene (also known as buckyballs) is fairly common, and can be found in soot particles.

LIQUID POWER
Most gasoline molecules are chains, containing between five and ten carbon atoms. The gasoline molecule octane (left) contains eight carbons. Gasoline is derived from petroleum oil, a mixture of liquids, solids, and gases that are the fossilized remains of microscopic life.

Living matter

ANIMALS AND PLANTS ARE AMAZINGLY complex forms of living matter. They can grow, reproduce, move, and respond to their environments. Until the late 19th century, many scientists thought a "vital principle" must control the behavior of living matter. Such beliefs changed when scientists began to be able to synthesize a range of "organic" substances (substances previously found only in living things), and started to explain the chemistry of the processes within living creatures. It was once thought that flies and other small creatures could develop spontaneously from rotting matter, but Louis Pasteur (1822-1895) showed that new life can only arise from existing organisms. Life has never yet been made in a scientific laboratory from nonliving matter. This leaves the problem of how life developed on earth from a "soup" of nonliving molecules.

FLIES IN THE SOUP
In the 1860s, when Louis Pasteur boiled a flask of broth and left i[...] he learned that new lif[...] arises only from living matter. Dust from the air fell in the broth, an[...] microorganisms grew. But when only dust-fre[...] air reached the broth, nothing grew.

ANALYSING THE ORGANIC
In the 19th century many "organic" substances were closely examined. This apparatus (left) was used in the 1880s to measure the nitrogen in urea.

UNDERSTANDING UREA
A landmark in understanding life was the synthesis of urea, a nitrogen-containing chemical found in animal waste. Friedrich Wöhler (1800-1882) made urea in 1828 from ammonia and cyanic acid.

Saturated solution of common salt was placed in glass cup

Measuring tube was filled with distilled water

Central tube

Sodium hypobromite solution was placed in here

When the tap was opened, the solutions mixed, and nitrogen was produced and collected in the measuring tube

Sample of urea containing unknown concentration of nitrogen was placed in here

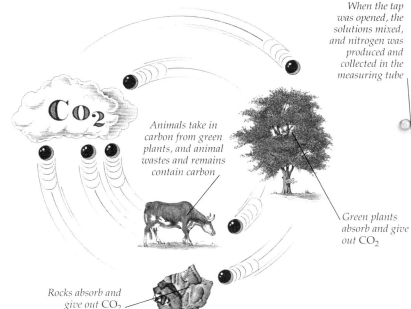

Animals take in carbon from green plants, and animal wastes and remains contain carbon

Green plants absorb and give out CO_2

Rocks absorb and give out CO_2

NEVERENDING CYCLE
Carbon is the basis for all living matter, circulating between air, oceans, rocks, and living things. Carbon dioxide gas (CO_2) is absorbed from the air by green plants. Plant-eaters use the plant's carbon for tissue-building. Carbon is returned to the environment in animals' waste products, and when dead animals decay. Rocks and water also absorb and give off CO_2 and complete the cycle.

Rods represent
chemical bonds

Meeting points of rods
represent atoms

SOLVING THE PUZZLE
In 1953 American James Watson (1928-) and Englishman
Francis Crick (1916-) discovered a vital clue to the secret of
living matter – the structure of DNA (deoxyribonucleic
acid). This substance, found in living cells, passes genetic
"information" from parents to offspring. DNA has two
chains of atoms linked in a double helix (like a spiral
staircase). The "stairs" are groups of atoms called bases.
The sequence of bases spells out the genetic "message."

Aluminum plates
represent the four
different bases

One of 20
triangular faces,
forming a
protective
protein "shell"

Model of
adenovirus

BUILDING THE GENETIC CODE
This model of DNA was originally
made in the 1950s by Watson and
Crick. It comprises a large
number of repeated structures,
and represents the information
needed to build and maintain
a living organism.

Protein
"spike"

ALIEN INVADER
Viruses lie on the
borderline between
the living and the
nonliving. They can
reproduce only by
invading a cell and
altering its DNA. The
cell then becomes a
factory for making
more viruses.

Sugar molecules (five-sided
groups of atoms) form
DNA's "backbone"

DNA
double
helix

EARLIEST ACID
These are highly
magnified crystals of
glycine, an amino acid.
There are about 20 amino
acids found in nearly all
living things. Glycine was
probably the first amino acid
to be formed in the "soup" of
nonliving molecules (also
known as the primordial soup).

DNA structure repeats
itself in a helix

Each strand contains
genetic information

Designing molecules

Artificial teeth and dental plate from the 1870s

IN THE MID-19TH CENTURY chemists began to use their new knowledge of organic molecules (pp. 42-43) to make new materials with valuable properties. Parkesine, an imitation ivory, was made in 1862 by Alexander Parkes (1813-1890). In 1884 Hilaire de Chardonnet (1839-1924) made rayon, the first artificial fiber, by imitating the chemical structure of silk. Rubber was toughened and made more useful by the vulcanizing process (heat treatment with sulfur), invented in 1839. The age of plastics was ushered in by Leo Baekeland (1863-1944), who invented Bakelite in 1909. Plastics are polymers – large molecules with possibly thousands of identical groups of atoms chained together. Plastics can be molded by heat and pressure, but then become fixed in shape. They are unreactive, and do not disturb the body's chemistry when used as a replacement hipjoint, for example. Plastics pose a waste disposal problem, however, for most are not biodegradable. In addition to plastics, modern chemists have designed many useful products, such as drugs, detergents, and alloys.

Matte bakelite

BAEKELAND'S BAKELITE
The first entirely synthetic plastic, bakelite was used in early telephones and other electrical devices. It was developed in the United States in 1909.

EBONITE ARTIFACT
This saxophone mouthpiece is made of ebonite, a type of vulcanized rubber. It is also known as vulcanite.

Ebonite resembles ebony

Alluring...Enduring...

Bakelite hairdryer

RUBBER WEAR
The synthetic rubber isoprene was made in 1892. It is much more resistant to wear than natural rubber. It became very important to the Allies during the Second World War, when rubber plantations in Southeast Asia were captured by the Japanese.

SILK SUBSTITUTE
Nylon, an artificial fiber that could be spun and woven, was first mass-produced in the 1940s. It was mainly used in stockings and underwear.

FLEXIBLE HARDNESS
These billiard balls are made of celluloid, a hard plastic. It is also flexible, and was used as a base for photographic film, and in shirt collars.

Samples of isoprene

BALATA BALL
Balata, a hard, rubberlike substance, is used for the outer casing of golf balls. Natural balata is now extremely rare, and has had to be replaced by synthetic plastics.

Outer casing of a golf ball is made of balata

IN THE FRAME
A tough high-density form of polyethylene is used for spectacle frames. Polyethylene is most familiar as packaging.

MARBLED FOUNTAIN
Plastic cases made fountainpens cheaper. Their "marbled" appearance was created by mixing different colored plastics.

PLASTIC PLATTER
This plastic plate is a thermoset – it has been hardened by heating during its manufacture, and is consequently heat-resistant.

Slightly marbled bakelite

HOT STUFF
Bakelite is a good thermal and electrical insulator, and was used in items such as this 1930s hairdryer.

PLASTIC PERSONALITY
The plastic Michelin Man advertises Michelin car tires, which are made of vulcanized rubber.

SCREEN TEST
Chemists now work with molecules on computer screens. This is a molecule of enkephalin, a natural substance in the brain that affects the perception of pain. The atoms in the molecule are color-coded, positioned, and in their correct proportions. Their positions can be modified, or new groups can be added. The computer has stored information about the forces between the atoms (pp. 60-61), so chemically impossible groupings are not permitted. The proposed molecule can be rigorously tested on screen, and precious laboratory research time can be saved.

Radioactivity

I<small>N 1880 THE ATOM WAS STILL THOUGHT TO BE</small> impenetrable and unchanging. However, by 1900 this picture was seen to be incorrect. An important new discovery was radioactivity. This is the emission of invisible radiations by certain kinds of atoms, happening spontaneously and unaffected by chemical reactions, temperature, or physical factors. The radiations are alpha, beta, or gamma (α, β, or γ). Ernest Rutherford (1871-1937) did most to clarify radioactivity. He found that α-particles were helium atoms, without electrons (pp. 48-49) and β-particles were fast electrons. When α- or β-particles were shot out from the atom, a different sort of atom was left. Such changes could cause γ-radiation, a type of electromagnetic radiation, to be emitted. Transmutation, long dreamed of by the alchemists as they tried to change one element into another, really was possible. It is now known that radiations in large doses, or in small exposures over long periods, can cause sickness and death. Nevertheless, radioactivity has many important uses. For example metal objects can be "X-rayed" with γ-rays, medicines moving around the body can be tagged with radioactive "tracers," and archaeological finds can be dated by measuring their radioactivity.

BECQUEREL'S RAYS
While studying Xrays (radiation that could penetrate certain materials) Antoine Becquerel (1852-1908) stumbled on a new kind of invisible, penetrating radiation. In 1896 he found that crystals of a uranium compound could "fog" photographic film, even when the film was wrapped in black paper.

Cartoon of the Curies

A CURIOUS COUPLE
Marie Curie (1867-1934), assisted by her husband Pierre (1859-1906), found that the uranium ore pitchblende was considerably more radioactive than pure uranium. They realized that pitchblende must contain additional, more highly radioactive substances. In 1902, after four years of laborious effort, they isolated tiny quantities of two new elements, polonium and radium. Like other early scientists working with radioactivity, the Curies knew little of its dangers, and Marie Curie died of leukemia. The high radiation levels with which she worked are evident from her glass flask – exposure to radiation turned it from clear to blue.

URANIUM ORE
Pitchblende is a brownish-black rock consisting mainly of uranium chemically combined with oxygen. It forms crystals called uraninite. Once considered useless, pitchblende is now the main source of uranium and radium.

Marie Curie's glass flask

FLASH GADGET
William Crookes (p. 48) invented the spinthariscope for detecting α-particles. The α-particles struck a screen coated with zinc sulfide, creating a tiny flash seen through the eyepiece.

GEIGER'S GAUGE
Hans Geiger (1882-1945) gave this Geiger counter, a device for measuring radiation levels, to James Chadwick (pp. 52-53) in 1932. In this early model, low-pressure gas is contained in a copper cylinder, fitted with a handle. An electrical voltage is applied between this casing and a thin wire running along its center. When an α- or β-particle enters the counter through a window at one end, it generates a brief burst of electric current between the case and the wire, which is detected on the counter.

Copper casing

Mica window

Thin wire runs the length of the counter

Insulated handle

Screw terminal

Connector

RADIATION OF THE ROCKS
A low level of "background" radioactivity is present in everything, even in our bodies. Levels are higher in regions of granite rock, for granite contains uranium. Granite emits radon gas, which can accumulate in homes and threaten health.

RADIOACTIVE SOLUTION
As part of his research into the transmutation of elements, Frederick Soddy (1877-1956) prepared this uranyl nitrate in 1905. It contains uranium and radium, and is highly radioactive. Its bright color is typical of uranium compounds.

Engraving on the flask reveals that the liquid contains 255 g of purified uranium, and 16×10^{-12} g of radium

PHYSICISTS AT WORK
Ernest Rutherford (right) and Hans Geiger in their laboratory at Manchester University in England, about 1908, with apparatus for detecting α-particles. Geiger and Rutherford realized that α-particles were helium atoms without electrons.

Part of image on shroud

CARBON DATING THE TURIN SHROUD
The body of the crucified Christ was reputedly wrapped in a shroud, and was said to have created a life-size image still visible on the cloth. Analysis of a radioactive form of carbon taken from tiny samples of the shroud, now kept at Turin, showed that in fact the cloth was from medieval times.

Container for shroud sample

Archbishop of Turin's seal

Inside the atom

THE FIRST CLUE TO THE STRUCTURE of the atom came from experiments by English physicist J. J. Thomson (1856-1940) in 1897. He discovered particles that were smaller than atoms in cathode rays. These rays were seen passing between high voltage terminals in a glass tube filled with low pressure gas. The particles, called corpuscles by Thomson and later known as electrons, had a negative electric charge and were about 2,000 times lighter than a hydrogen atom. They were exactly the same whatever gas was used in the tube, and whatever metal the terminals were made of. This strongly suggested that electrons were present in all matter. Atoms must also contain positive electric charge to balance the negative charge of electrons. Ernest Rutherford (pp. 46-47) probed atoms with particles produced in his radioactivity experiments, and found that the positive charge was concentrated in a tiny nucleus. He reached the conclusion that the atom resembled a miniature solar system, where the "planets" were the electrons and the "sun" was the nucleus.

Paper scale for measuring deflection of electron beam

Low-pressure gas

High voltage between the metal plates creates an electric field, which bends the paths of charged particles

Particles make glowing spot on glass

ATOM ATTACK
In 1911 Ernest Rutherford studied the effects of bombarding pieces of gold or platinum foil with alpha (α) particles – positively charged particles given out by radioactive materials (pp. 46-47). Most α– particles passed through the foil, but about one in 8,000 was deflected by more than 90°. Rutherford explained that this was due to the nucleus – a dense center of positive charge within the atom.

Positively charged nucleus

α–particle deflected by more than 90°

α–particle scarcely deviated

α–particle track strongly bent

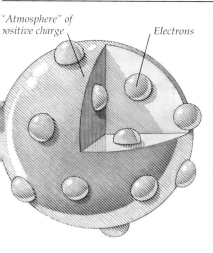

"Atmosphere" of positive charge

Electrons

THOMSON'S DISCOVERIES

J. J. Thomson intended to be an engineer, but instead became a brilliant physicist. He studied cathode rays with great success because he managed to achieve very low gas pressures in his modified Crookes tube. Thomson's discovery of the electron – the fundamental unit of electric current, present in all matter – revolutionized the theories of electricity and atoms. He also confirmed the existence of isotopes (pp. 52-53) – elements that each have several types of atoms, chemically identical, but differing in weight.

THE PLUM PUDDING ATOM

In his plum pudding theory, J. J. Thomson suggested that every atom consists of a number of electrons, and an amount of positive charge to balance their negative charges. He thought the positive charge formed an "atmosphere" through which the electrons moved, like plums in a plum pudding.

Electrons pass through slits in anodes (positive terminal)

Heated cathode (negative terminal) produces electrons

WEIGHING THE ELECTRON

This is Thomson's original apparatus for studying cathode rays. It contained low pressure gas, through which cathode rays passed. The paths of the rays were bent by an electric field and Thomson measured the amount of bending. The electric field was switched off, a magnetic field was switched on, and again the bending was measured. Thomson calculated that if the particles had the same charge as the hydrogen ion (an "incomplete" atom) found in electrolysis (pp. 50-51) they must be about 2,000 times lighter.

Coils for magnetic field, which bends the charged particles

Negatively charged electron

RUTHERFORD'S DISCOVERIES

During his experiments with radioactivity, Ernest Rutherford discovered the transmutation (p. 46) of one element into another. He also studied the half-life of an element – the time taken for half of a sample of a radioactive element to decay, or change into another element. He published his discoveries in 1904 in his book *Radioactivity*.

THE NUCLEAR ATOM

After Rutherford's explanation of the scattering of α–particles, the structure of the atom became clearer. Negatively charged electrons were thought to move around a positively charged, dense nucleus, much like planets moving around the sun. However, there were problems with this "solar-system" model. According to the laws of physics at that time, such an atom should have collapsed instantly in a burst of electromagnetic radiation. (It is now known that the atom does not collapse because electrons are only "allowed" certain energies, pp. 50-51.)

Positively charged nucleus

Electrons, shells, and bonds

IN THE EARLY 1900S the structure of the atom became clearer, but the laws of physics at the time could not explain why electrons did not quickly spiral in toward the nucleus. Niels Bohr (1885-1962), a student of Rutherford, helped to solve the mystery by suggesting that electrons were only "allowed" certain energies. He found that electrons with the lowest allowed energy orbit closest to the nucleus, and electrons with the highest allowed energy orbit furthest away. It was soon discovered that there is a limit to the number of electrons with each energy. Electrons in an atom behave as if they are stacked, lowest energies first, in "shells" around the nucleus. It is the electrons in an atom's outermost shell that decide an atom's chemical properties. Atoms with outer shells "filled" with electrons are less reactive than those with only one electron in their outer shell. The outermost electrons join, or bond, with other atoms to form molecules. This new picture of the atom explained the reactions of atoms in processes such as electrolysis.

THE EXPENSE OF EROS
In 1884 this aluminum statue of the Greek god Eros was highly expensive, but now aluminum can be cheaply produced by electrolysis.

LIBERATING LAWS
Michael Faraday (1791-1867) discovered the laws of electrolysis in 1832. He found that elements are liberated by a certain amount of electricity, or by twice or three times this amount. This depends on the number of outer electrons.

Terminal

Electrons flow into the carbon plate

Zinc plate could be lifted out of the chromic acid to switch off the current

Carbon plate

Electrons flow out of the zinc plate and around the electrical circuit connected to the terminals

Carbon plate

Glass jar was filled with chromic acid

ELECTRON STREAMS
Electric cells like this "bichromate cell" could be joined together to make a battery. The plates of carbon and zinc react with the chromic acid in the glass jar, transferring a stream of electrons from the zinc to the carbon.

ELECTRIFYING DISCOVERIES
In the 19th century many new elements were discovered by passing electric current through solutions or molten materials. The samples of metals shown here were prepared by electrolysis, and the electric current came from a battery. Electrolysis can separate compounds into elements by supplying electrons to, or removing them from, the outer shells of atoms.

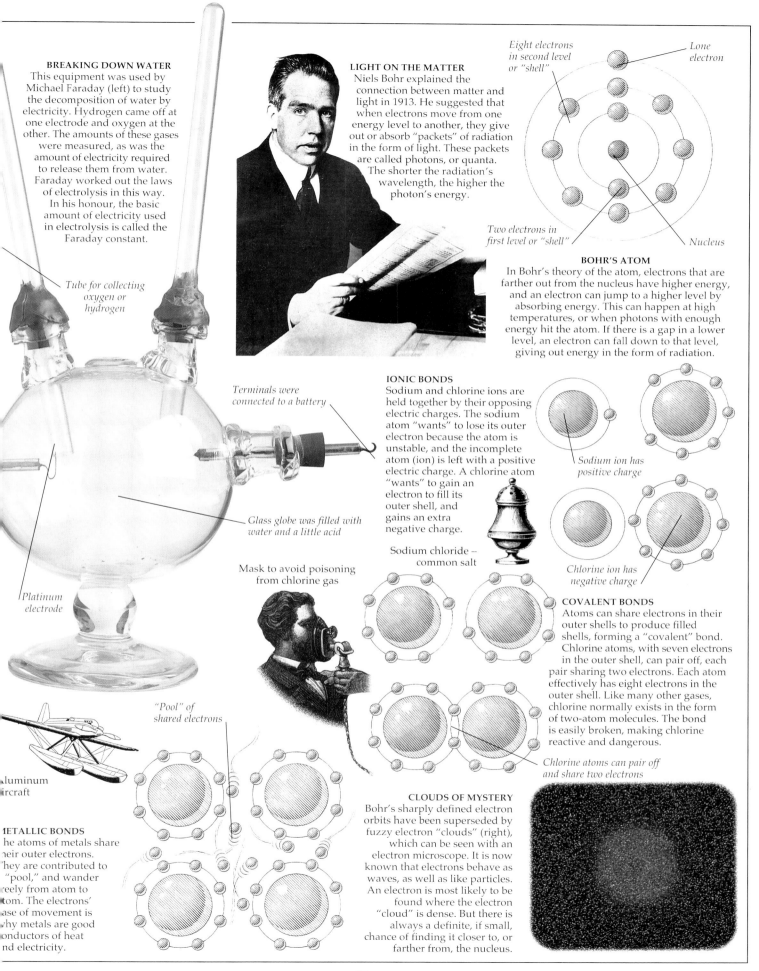

BREAKING DOWN WATER

This equipment was used by Michael Faraday (left) to study the decomposition of water by electricity. Hydrogen came off at one electrode and oxygen at the other. The amounts of these gases were measured, as was the amount of electricity required to release them from water. Faraday worked out the laws of electrolysis in this way. In his honour, the basic amount of electricity used in electrolysis is called the Faraday constant.

Tube for collecting oxygen or hydrogen

Platinum electrode

Terminals were connected to a battery

Glass globe was filled with water and a little acid

LIGHT ON THE MATTER

Niels Bohr explained the connection between matter and light in 1913. He suggested that when electrons move from one energy level to another, they give out or absorb "packets" of radiation in the form of light. These packets are called photons, or quanta. The shorter the radiation's wavelength, the higher the photon's energy.

Eight electrons in second level or "shell"

Lone electron

Two electrons in first level or "shell"

Nucleus

BOHR'S ATOM

In Bohr's theory of the atom, electrons that are farther out from the nucleus have higher energy, and an electron can jump to a higher level by absorbing energy. This can happen at high temperatures, or when photons with enough energy hit the atom. If there is a gap in a lower level, an electron can fall down to that level, giving out energy in the form of radiation.

IONIC BONDS

Sodium and chlorine ions are held together by their opposing electric charges. The sodium atom "wants" to lose its outer electron because the atom is unstable, and the incomplete atom (ion) is left with a positive electric charge. A chlorine atom "wants" to gain an electron to fill its outer shell, and gains an extra negative charge.

Sodium ion has positive charge

Chlorine ion has negative charge

Sodium chloride – common salt

Mask to avoid poisoning from chlorine gas

COVALENT BONDS

Atoms can share electrons in their outer shells to produce filled shells, forming a "covalent" bond. Chlorine atoms, with seven electrons in the outer shell, can pair off, each pair sharing two electrons. Each atom effectively has eight electrons in the outer shell. Like many other gases, chlorine normally exists in the form of two-atom molecules. The bond is easily broken, making chlorine reactive and dangerous.

Chlorine atoms can pair off and share two electrons

"Pool" of shared electrons

luminum ircraft

METALLIC BONDS

The atoms of metals share their outer electrons. They are contributed to a "pool," and wander freely from atom to atom. The electrons' ease of movement is why metals are good conductors of heat and electricity.

CLOUDS OF MYSTERY

Bohr's sharply defined electron orbits have been superseded by fuzzy electron "clouds" (right), which can be seen with an electron microscope. It is now known that electrons behave as waves, as well as like particles. An electron is most likely to be found where the electron "cloud" is dense. But there is always a definite, if small, chance of finding it closer to, or farther from, the nucleus.

Architecture of the nucleus

By the early 20th century, it was known that the atom had a positively charged nucleus. Ernest Rutherford (pp. 46-47) suggested that the nucleus contained positively charged particles called "protons" (Greek for "first things"). He demonstrated their existence in 1919 by knocking them out of nitrogen nuclei using alpha (α) particles. James Chadwick (1891-1974) discovered another particle in the nucleus in 1932 – the neutron, an uncharged particle of about the same mass as the proton. All nuclei comprise protons and neutrons. The number of protons determines the number of electrons circling the nucleus, and therefore the chemical properties of the atom (pp. 50-51). All elements have different isotopes – atoms with the same number of protons but different numbers of neutrons.

PARTICLE DISCOVERER
James Chadwick, a student of Rutherford, discovered neutrons by exposing the metal beryllium to α-particles. He observed a new kind of particle ejected from its nucleus, the neutron. Later he studied deuterium (also known as "heavy hydrogen"). This isotope of hydrogen was discovered in 1932 and is used in nuclear reactors.

Ions separated by mass and charge strike film and create image

Magnetic field inside the electromagnet deflects particles

Beam of particles passes along this tube

Low-pressure gas

Ions of particular kind are produced here

Anode (positive terminal)

SEPARATING ISOTOPES
This was the first mass spectrograph, designed by F. W. Aston (1877-1945). It could separate isotopes – chemically identical atoms with different masses. The globe contained a compound of the material to be tested, either as part of the anode (positive terminal) or as low-pressure gas. An electric current knocked electrons from the material's atoms, leaving positively charged ions that passed through a collecting slit. The beam of charged particles was bent by an electric field and then by a magnetic one. It was spread into separate bands on a photographic film, according to the ions' charge and mass.

Electrons, protons, and neutrons

Rutherford believed the nucleus was made up of protons and a smaller number of electrons. He thought that each electron was closely paired with a proton to make a "doublet" that was neutral (had zero electric charge). In 1932 James Chadwick produced a type of radiation that did not bend in an electric field, but was far more penetrating than gamma rays. This radiation consisted of uncharged particles, known as "neutrons," that were about as massive as hydrogen atoms. Chadwick realized that these neutrons might be particles themselves, and not a proton and electron combined. This view is now accepted. However, a free neutron has a 50 percent chance of "decaying" into a proton and electron in 15 minutes. If a proton and electron collide they will produce a neutron.

NEUTRON DETECTOR
Inside this intriguing apparatus built by Chadwick, α-particles from a radioactive source struck a beryllium target. The neutrons given off could be detected only when they knocked protons from a piece of paraffin wax. The protons were detected with a Geiger counter (pp. 46-47).

Tube was fixed to an air pump to take air out of the chamber

Chamber contained a radioactive source

A SCIENTIST'S TOOLS
This cigarette carton was Chadwick's "toolbox." He used the pieces of paraffin wax to observe neutrons. The silver and aluminum foils, of different thicknesses, were used as barriers to determine the penetrating power of the radiation.

Power supply

One of six orbiting electrons – negative charge

CARBON-12
The chemical properties of carbon are determined by its six negatively charged electrons. These six electrons balance the six positively charged protons of the nucleus. In a carbon-12 atom, the nucleus also has six neutrons, of about the same mass as the protons, giving the atom a "mass number" of 12.

One of six protons – positive charge

One of six neutrons – zero charge

One of six orbiting electrons – negative charge

CARBON-14
The isotope carbon-14 is chemically identical to ordinary carbon. It has six protons and six electrons. But carbon-14 has two extra neutrons, giving it a mass number of 14. This isotope is radioactive, 50 percent of it decaying every 5,730 years. Environmental levels are roughly constant, since new carbon-14 atoms are constantly being formed by cosmic rays smashing into ordinary carbon atoms.

One of six protons – positive charge

One of eight neutrons – zero charge

Splitting the atom

AFTER THE DISCOVERY of the nucleus in 1911, it was found that bombarding certain atoms with particles from radioactive materials could disintegrate their nuclei, releasing energy. The heaviest nuclei, those of uranium, can be split by neutrons in this way. Otto Hahn (1879-1968) and Lise Meitner (1878-1968) discovered that the uranium nucleus splits in half, or "fissions," and also gives out further neutrons. These neutrons can go on to cause further fissions. In 1942 a team led by Enrico Fermi (1901-1954) achieved this "chain reaction" in the world's first nuclear reactor. Three years later the chain reaction was used in the nuclear bombs that destroyed the Japanese cities of Hiroshima and Nagasaki.

Neutrons produced by fission

Typical products of fission are barium and krypton

Nucleus fissions into two smaller nuclei

CHAIN REACTION
The source of energy in a nuclear reactor or a nuclear explosion is a chain reaction. A nucleus of uranium or plutonium splits (fissions), giving out neutrons that split further nuclei. Immense heat is created by the energy of the splitting fragments and by radiation. In a reactor this heat is used in a controlled way to generate electricity. In an explosion it is released violently.

Neutron about to hit uranium nucleus

1 WANDERING NEUTRONS
Neutrons can be released by bombarding atoms with radiation. Neutrons are also occasionally given out by decaying uranium nuclei, but these neutrons rarely react with uranium nuclei to build a chain reaction. Many nuclear reactors use uranium-235, a very reactive but uncommon isotope.

2 NUCLEAR SPLIT
When a neutron hits another uranium nucleus, the nucleus fissions into two smaller nuclei of approximately half the size. Several neutrons are also given out, together with high-energy radiation. The neutrons can go on to cause further fissions in a chain reaction. Neutrons can be slowed down by graphite or heavy water mixed with the uranium.

Uranium nucleus (U-235)

Unstable uranium

The main isotope of uranium is uranium-238 (symbol U-238). It has 238 particles in its nucleus – 92 protons and 146 neutrons. The neutrons prevent the protons from blowing the nucleus apart because of their mutual repulsion. Even so, an unstable U-238 nucleus breaks down from time to time, giving out an alpha (α) particle and turning into a thorium nucleus. The thorium nucleus in turn breaks down, and so do its products, in a chain of decays that ends when a lead nucleus is formed. Other uranium isotopes go through a similar chain of radioactive decays, ending in a different isotope of lead. This is why uranium-bearing rocks can be detected by their radioactivity. Uranium can also break down by fission, and this process can build up into a chain reaction. For a chain reaction to occur, there must be special conditions, and a sufficient quantity of relatively pure uranium must be used.

FAMILY FISSION
In 1917 Lise Meitner and Otto Hahn discovered a new element, protactinium, found in uranium ores. In 1939 Meitner and her nephew Otto Frisch (1904-1979) announced the fission of uranium.

PUZZLING PRODUCT
Otto Hahn studied the disintegration of uranium nuclei by neutrons. Among the by-products of this disintegration were barium nuclei, which are about half the weight of uranium nuclei.

HEAVY WATER
Neutrons in a nuclear reactor's chain reaction can be controlled by a moderator such as heavy water. It is 11 percent heavier than an equal volume of ordinary water.

PROPHET OF THE BOMB
In 1905, 40 years before the first nuclear explosion, Albert Einstein (1879-1955) showed in his Theory of Special Relativity that energy and mass can be converted into each other. In 1939 he warned President Franklin Roosevelt that a uranium chain reaction could be used in a powerful new bomb.

RODS IN THE REACTOR
These fuel rods are used in Magnox nuclear reactors. The rods consist of long bars of natural uranium, clad in magnox, a magnesium alloy. In the reactor carbon dioxide gas flows around the rods, carrying away the generated heat.

Single pellet of uranium oxide

A RICHER FUEL
This fuel rod contains pellets of a compound of uranium, uranium dioxide, containing a high proportion of uranium-235. These rods are used in the Magnox reactor and the British Advanced Gas-cooled Reactor (AGR).

Fuel rods are about 5 ft (about 5 m) long

BLOW-UP
In an atomic explosion pieces of uranium or plutonium are hurled together by explosives to form a chain reaction. In the explosion a very tiny amount of matter completely disappears (p. 28).

BOMB BUILDER
J. Robert Oppenheimer (1904-1967) joined the US atomic bomb project in 1942, and was director of the laboratory that built the first nuclear bombs. His atomic research ended when his security clearance was withdrawn in 1954.

LIGHT AT THE CORE
The eerie blue glow in the heart of this nuclear reactor is called Cherenkov radiation. It is caused by electrons from radioactive fuel plowing through water and giving out light. The chain reaction in a nuclear reactor can be controlled by rods containing a neutron-absorbing material such as cadmium. The intense heat of the reactor's core is carried away by gas, liquid metal, or high-pressure water.

Hot matter

Atoms are laid bare as they are subjected to high temperatures. The spectroscope reveals their secrets by analyzing the light they give out. In a spectroscope the light falls on a diffraction grating – a flat surface with thousands of lines – or a prism. Light passes through or is reflected, and is broken up into different colors. Sunlight consists of the whole color spectrum and beyond. Gases at the sun's surface produce sunlight, at temperatures of about 10,000° F (about 5,500° C). Here, the atoms' outer electrons are knocked to higher orbits and give out light as they fall back (pp. 50-51). Inside the sun and other high-temperature stars, inner electrons are knocked to higher orbits. As they fall back, they give out ultraviolet and X-rays. At the centers of the sun and stars, at temperatures of about 27 million° F (around 15 million° C), nuclei are stripped bare and welded together, producing heavier nuclei.

INSIDE THE PLASMA BALL
A powerful voltage at the center of this glass globe tears electrons from the atoms of the low-pressure gases inside. Avalanches of electrons build up, forming bright squiggly lines of hot gas. The mixture of electrons and charged atoms in these lines is called a plasma.

A LIGHT SIGNATURE
The spectrometer "reads the signature" of materials by analyzing their light. The light first passes through a narrow slit into a small telescope, which focuses the light into a narrow parallel beam. The beam passes through a glass prism, and is spread out, with each wavelength (color) of light going in a slightly different direction. Through a viewing telescope a rainbow-colored "spectrum" can be seen. This may appear as a host of bright lines, or a continuous band of color, crossed by dark lines, where wavelengths have been absorbed.

Photographic plate

Plateholder

Camera

THE VANISHING SUN
The sun is kept at a high temperature by the flood of energy from the nuclear reactions at its heart. Every second, four million tons of the sun's matter vanish, converted into energy that escapes from the surface as radiation.

ABSORBING EXPERIMENT
This 19th-century spectroscopic experiment shows light from a gas flame passing through a liquid containing dissolved materials. The spectrum that is produced reveals the identity of the dissolved materials in the liquid.

Building nuclei by fusion

Merging (fusing) light nuclei yields an immense amount of energy. Hydrogen has the very lightest nucleus, containing just one proton. Hydrogen nuclei can be fused to form one nucleus of helium (two of the protons are turned into neutrons, forming a helium nucleus with two protons and two neutrons). Energy is given out at the same time. This fusion process takes place in the sun and stars in a series of stages, with other nuclei forming briefly, then changing into other nuclei. On earth, hydrogen isotopes such as deuterium and tritium are used for fusion. The supply of deuterium, also known as heavy hydrogen, is limitless, because it is found in the ocean.

HARNESSING FUSION
At temperatures of millions of degrees, electrons are completely stripped from atoms. Light nuclei such as hydrogen can collide, despite the mutual repulsion of their positive electric charges. The fusion of hydrogen nuclei to form helium nuclei powers the sun, a hydrogen bomb, and the prospective fusion reactors of the future.

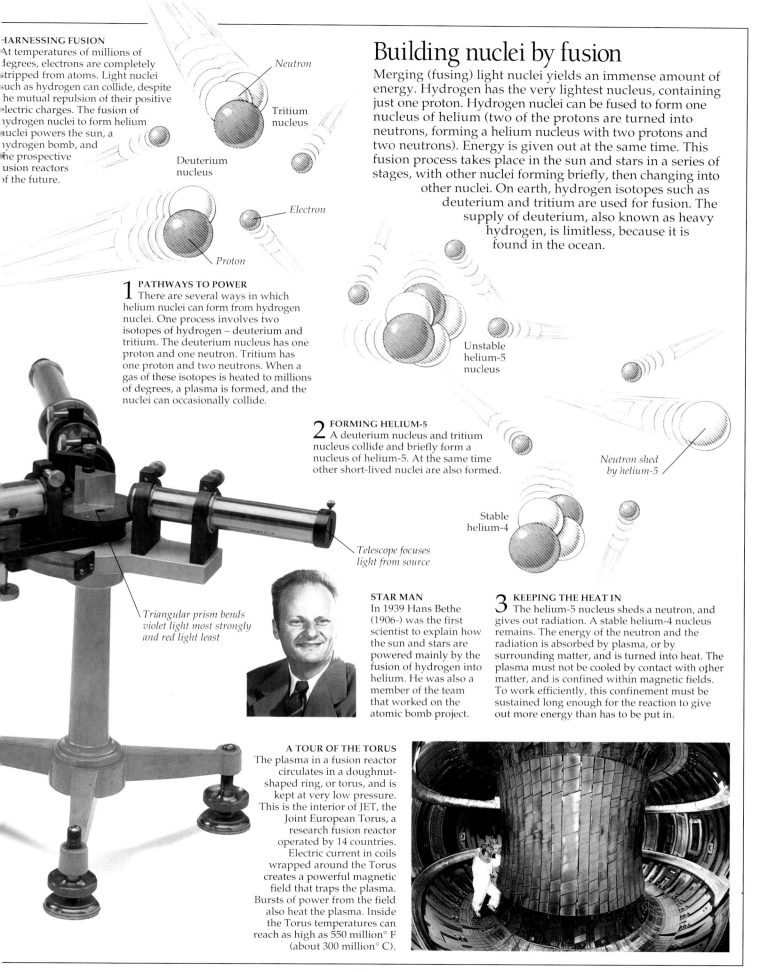

Neutron

Tritium nucleus

Deuterium nucleus

Electron

Proton

1 PATHWAYS TO POWER
There are several ways in which helium nuclei can form from hydrogen nuclei. One process involves two isotopes of hydrogen – deuterium and tritium. The deuterium nucleus has one proton and one neutron. Tritium has one proton and two neutrons. When a gas of these isotopes is heated to millions of degrees, a plasma is formed, and the nuclei can occasionally collide.

Unstable helium-5 nucleus

2 FORMING HELIUM-5
A deuterium nucleus and tritium nucleus collide and briefly form a nucleus of helium-5. At the same time other short-lived nuclei are also formed.

Neutron shed by helium-5

Stable helium-4

Telescope focuses light from source

Triangular prism bends violet light most strongly and red light least

STAR MAN
In 1939 Hans Bethe (1906-) was the first scientist to explain how the sun and stars are powered mainly by the fusion of hydrogen into helium. He was also a member of the team that worked on the atomic bomb project.

3 KEEPING THE HEAT IN
The helium-5 nucleus sheds a neutron, and gives out radiation. A stable helium-4 nucleus remains. The energy of the neutron and the radiation is absorbed by plasma, or by surrounding matter, and is turned into heat. The plasma must not be cooled by contact with other matter, and is confined within magnetic fields. To work efficiently, this confinement must be sustained long enough for the reaction to give out more energy than has to be put in.

A TOUR OF THE TORUS
The plasma in a fusion reactor circulates in a doughnut-shaped ring, or torus, and is kept at very low pressure. This is the interior of JET, the Joint European Torus, a research fusion reactor operated by 14 countries. Electric current in coils wrapped around the Torus creates a powerful magnetic field that traps the plasma. Bursts of power from the field also heat the plasma. Inside the Torus temperatures can reach as high as 550 million° F (about 300 million° C).

Subatomic particles

IN THE EARLY 1930s the atom was thought to be made of three kinds of particle – the proton, neutron, and electron. But soon more particles were found. The existence of the neutrino – a ghostlike particle that "carries away" energy when a neutron decays (p. 53) – was suspected. Then the muon, much like a heavy electron, and the pion, which binds protons and neutrons together in the nucleus, were both discovered in cosmic rays. Accelerators were built to smash particles into nuclei at high speed, creating new particles. Today hundreds of particles are known. They seem to fall into two main classes, hadrons and leptons. Hadrons include the proton and neutron, and are made of pairs or triplets of quarks, which are never seen singly. Leptons, the other class, include electrons and neutrinos.

MAKING TRACKS
Trails of water droplets in a cloud chamber mark the paths of electrons and positrons (similar to an electron but with a positive charge). Because of their opposite electric charges, they curve in different directions in the chamber's magnetic field. An electron produced near the bottom of the picture circles 36 times before losing its energy.

Chamber contains water vapor

The piston at the bottom of the chamber moves to form water vapor which condenses on the tracks of particles as they pass through

AMAZING REVELATIONS
The cloud chamber, invented by Charles Wilson (1869-1959) in 1911, was the first detector to reveal subatomic particles in flight. Particles from a radioactive source pass through a glass chamber, which contains air and water vapor. In the glass chamber, particles knock electrons out of the atoms in the air, leaving positively charged ions (incomplete atoms). The pressure in the chamber is suddenly reduced, and water vapor condenses on the ions, forming trails of small drops.

To lower the piston the flask is emptied of air – the connection between the flask and the space below the piston is opened and the piston is suddenly sucked downward

Glass negatives of cloud chamber photographs

PARTICLE PICTURES
Photographic plates of cloud chamber tracks often show particles being created and destroyed. Measuring the tracks can reveal the particles' electric charge, mass, and speed.

Vacuum tank is sealed and the air is removed

IN A WHIRL
The cyclotron, invented by Ernest Lawrence (1901-1958) in 1930, accelerated particles and smashed them into atomic nuclei to form new particles. The vacuum tank of the cyclotron shown here housed a metal "dee" (a D-shaped box). Charged particles entered the dee at the center of the apparatus, and a magnetic field moved them in a small circle, half in and half out of the dee. A rapidly varying electric voltage was applied to the dee, giving a "kick" to a particle whenever it left or reentered the dee. The particle spiraled outward, traveling faster and faster, until it left the cyclotron.

"Dee"

The vacuum tank of the cyclotron

Source of protons

JESTER OF PHYSICS
Richard Feynman (1918-1988) shared a Nobel Prize in 1965 for his work on the forces between particles and electromagnetic radiation. He was considered a brilliant teacher and was famous for his practical jokes.

Photon is exchanged by electrons

Electron

Electron

A   B

FEYNMAN DIAGRAM
This strange squiggle is a Feynman diagram. It illustrates that electromagnetic force between electrons occurs when they exchange a photon (the "carrier" of the electromagnetic force, pp. 60-61).

Bubble chamber contained liquid hydrogen

PARTICLE FROTH
This bubble chamber, made in 1956, contained liquid hydrogen at low temperature and high pressure. The pressure was suddenly released, and particles passed through the chamber. The liquid boiled on the trails of charged atoms left by the particles. The trails were photographed, and the chamber was quickly repressurized.

MAGIC CIRCLE
The underground Tevatron at the Fermi National Accelerator Laboratory in Illinois has two accelerators, one above the other. The upper one feeds particles to the more powerful lower one.

BEAUTY IN DECAY
In this computer graphic representation bubble-chamber image, a high-speed proton (yellow, bottom) collides with a proton in a hydrogen atom and disappears, creating a shower of particles. An uncharged particle called a lambda leaves no track, but reveals itself by "decaying" into a proton and a pion (yellow and purple, center).

"Porthole" for viewing tracks

When in use, the bubble chamber sat in this lower chamber and was kept at a low temperature

RECONSTRUCTING THE EVENT
Computers are now used to reconstruct subatomic events. This is a computer simulation of the decay of the Z^0 particle, one of the carriers of the weak nuclear force (pp. 60-61).

The four forces

NOT-SO-WEAK FORCE
The sun is powered by the weak nuclear force, which is responsible for the conversion of hydrogen into helium at the sun's core (p. 57). Under the less extreme conditions on earth, the weak nuclear force is involved in radioactivity. This force does not extend beyond the atomic nucleus and could not be detected until scientists had learned how to probe inside the atom. The particles that carry the weak force, the W^+, W^-, and Z^0, were discovered in 1983 among the debris formed when subatomic particles collided in a giant accelerator.

ALL MATTER IS SUBJECT TO four forces – gravity, electromagnetism, and the weak and strong nuclear forces. Gravity holds people on the earth and the planets in orbit around the sun. Electrons are held in atoms by electromagnetism, a force that is enormously stronger than gravity. The weak nuclear force, a hundred billion times weaker than electromagnetism, is involved in radioactivity and nuclear fusion (pp. 56-57). The strong nuclear force, a hundred times stronger than electromagnetism, affects particles called quarks. Protons, neutrons, and other particles are made up of pairs or triplets of quarks. Electromagnetism is "carried" by particles called photons, the weak nuclear force by W and Z particles, and the strong nuclear force by particles called gluons. Gravity is probably carried by particles, too – these have been dubbed gravitons. Electricity and magnetism are "unified" because electricity in motion produces magnetic fields, and changing magnetic fields produces electrical voltages. Electromagnetism is in turn unified with the weak nuclear force, because at extremely high energies and temperatures they merge into one "electro-weak" force. The evidence for this comes from ideas about the first moments of the Big Bang (pp. 62-63) and from experiments in particle accelerators. Physicists are now working to develop a theory in which all four forces would be aspects of one superforce.

Earth

Moon

Sun

An orrery, a mechanical model of planetary motions

PULLING POWER
Gravity is the force in control of the entire solar system – it holds planets, asteroids, comets, and smaller bodies in orbit. The farthest known planet, Pluto, is firmly held by gravity even when it is about 4 billion miles (over 7 billion kilometers) away from the sun. Gravity extends far beyond this, however – clusters of galaxies millions of light-years across are held together by their own gravity. Yet it is by far the weakest of the four forces. It dominates the universe because it is long-range, whereas the far stronger nuclear forces do not extend beyond the nucleus. Gravity is cumulative – it always attracts, never repels, so when matter accumulates into planet-sized or star-sized objects, a large gravitational force is developed. Electromagnetic forces are also long-range, but unlike gravity can both attract and repel, and generally cancel themselves out.

EVERYDAY INTERACTIONS

Many forces can be easily seen, such as the way materials hold together and the friction between objects. These are both examples of the electromagnetic force. Gravity is the other force that is most obvious in human life. The electromagnetic force and gravity are shown in the following sequence.

1 GETTING THINGS GOING

A ball falls to the floor because the earth's gravity pulls it, but the ball also pulls the earth with exactly the same force. However, since the earth has so much more mass, it does not move visibly, while the ball moves faster and faster. It is described as gaining energy of movement, or kinetic energy. Energy can be defined as making things happen – for example to break things, to make them hotter, and to set them in motion.

QUARK-FINDER

The strongest force of all, the strong nuclear force, is felt only by quarks. It binds them tightly together, and they have never yet been observed singly. During the 1980s evidence about the strong force carrying quarks, and the weak force, came from experiments in this giant accelerator, called the Super Proton Synchrotron.

EXCHANGING MESSAGES

When two particles are interacting through one of the four fundamental forces, they constantly exchange messenger particles. The messenger particles influence the other particles' movements the way a tennis ball influences the tennis players' movements. The force can be a repulsion or an attraction.

3 GREAT POTENTIAL

The potential energy that was momentarily stored in the ball is converted into kinetic energy, and the ball shoots upward. As the ball rises, it loses kinetic energy. If it should fall back to the ground later it will regain its speed. It is therefore described as converting kinetic into potential energy as it rises. In this case the potential energy is associated with height above the ground.

Gravity pulls the ball to the floor, but the ball pulls the earth with exactly the same force

Potential energy is converted into kinetic energy and the ball bounces up

DOWN WITH A BUMP

When the ball hits the floor, the force of gravity is opposed by electromagnetism. The electrons in the outer layers of atoms in the ball and the floor repel each other. The upward push of electromagnetism overcomes the downward pull of gravity. The motion is abruptly stopped, but the ball's kinetic energy is converted into other forms. Some is dispersed through the material of the ball and floor as heat. Some is stored as potential energy (energy waiting to be released) in the ball. The electromagnetic forces between the atoms are distorted by the impact, and try to restore the ball to its normal shape. When they succeed the ball regains its kinetic energy.

CONSTANT QUANTITY

In any isolated system the total quantity of mass and energy is conserved. In a steam engine, for example, chemical energy of the fuel is converted into heat energy of the fire and of the steam. This heat energy is in turn converted into kinetic energy of the wheels driven by the engine. The total amount of mass and energy is always conserved whichever of the four fundamental forces are involved.

The birth and death of matter

THE TOTAL AMOUNT of mass and energy in the universe never changes. According to a widely held theory, billions of years ago the universe contained matter and energy of extraordinarily high density and temperature, which exploded in the Big Bang. As the gas expanded and cooled, quarks formed protons and neutrons, and some of these built helium nuclei. Eventually complete hydrogen and helium atoms formed. The gas condensed into galaxy-sized clouds which broke up into stars. In the far future, the universe could collapse, be rejuvenated in a new Big Bang, and re-expand, but it is more likely that it will always expand. After the last star has faded, even protons may decay into much lighter particles, and the universe may end as a sea of electrons, neutrinos, and forms of radiation.

VIOLENT UNIVERSE
Early astronomers thought that the stars were tranquil and unchanging. It is now known, however, that they are born, lead violent lives, and die.

PUTTING THE CLOCK BACK
Time does not necessarily go forward, or even at the same speed. If the universe were to collapse, it is possible that time could go backward. Time slows down for high-speed objects – a person in orbit for a year ages less (by a hundredth of a second) than people on earth. Even time travel may be possible. In theory, two regions of the universe can be connected by a "wormhole," passing though other dimensions. An object entering one end of a wormhole could reappear from the other end, at an earlier time.

Time could go backward in the extreme conditions found in the cosmos

SCATTERED SEED
The Crab Nebula is a mass of gas from a supernova – the explosion of a giant star, seen by Chinese astronomers in 1054. The gas is rich in elements made in the star's core. These will be scattered through space and some will be incorporated into new planets as they are born. All the elements in our bodies were made in some ancient supernova.

THE GRAVITY OF DARK MATTER

Galaxies are huge collections of stars, gas, and dust. Light, travelling at about 200,000 miles (300,000 km) per second, can take as long as 100,000 years to cross a galaxy. Galaxies are grouped into clusters, which hurtle apart. There may be undetected dark matter in the vast spaces between galaxies. The gravity of dark matter may be sufficient to slow the galaxies' expansion and turn it into a collapse.

A BRIEF HISTORY OF BLACK HOLES

Stephen Hawking (1942-) is renowned for his work on explaining the birth of the universe and also for his theories about black holes. When matter becomes extremely dense, as in the core of an exploded star, its gravity becomes so powerful that both matter and radiation, including light, are trapped inside. The result is a black hole. Hawking showed that a black hole gives off radiation very slowly. His most popular work is the 1988 book *A Brief History of Time*.

AN INTELLIGENT UNIVERSE?

Fred Hoyle (1915-) is associated with the Steady State theory, which holds there was no Big Bang, and matter is always being created throughout space. He claims that some physical laws have been designed by a superior intelligence specifically to produce conditions that make the development of carbon-based life possible.

BACK TO THE BEGINNING

So far, the strongest evidence available to scientists for the Big Bang theory is cosmic background radiation. This is microwave radiation that can be detected by large radio telescopes like the one shown here. The radiation always comes with the same strength from all directions in the sky, and is believed by some to have traveled through space since the universe was 100,000 years old. Until this time the universe is thought to have been made of hot expanding plasma (pp. 56-57). The plasma then cooled sufficiently to allow electrons and nuclei to join up and form the first complete atoms.

Index

Acknowledgments

Dorling Kindersley would like to thank:
John Becklake, Chris Berridge, Tim Boon, Roger Bridgman, Neil Brown, Robert Bud, Sue Cackett, Ann Carter, Ann de Caires, Helen Dowling, Stewart Emmens, Robert Excell, Stephen Foulger, Graeme Fyffe, Derek Hudson, Kevin Johnson, Sarah Leonard, Steve Long, Stephanie Millard, Peter Morris, Keith Parker, David Ray and his staff, Anthony Richards, Derek Robinson, Victoria Smith, Peter Stephens, Laura Taylor, Peter Tomlinson, Denys Vaughan, Nicole Weisz, and Anthony Wilson for help with the provision of objects for photography; Jane Bull for design guidance; Deborah Rhodes for page makeup; Debra Clapson for editorial assistance; Marianna Papachrysanthou for design assistance; Neil Ardley for synopsis development; Stephen Pollock-Hill at Nazeing Glassworks for his expertise; Jane Burton, Jane Dickins, Paul Hammond, and Fiona Spence of De Beers for providing props.

Picture research Deborah Pownall and Catherine O'Rourke
Illustrations John Woodcock
Index Jane Parker

Picture credits

t=top b=bottom c=center l=left r=right

Bildarchiv Preussischer Kulturbesitz 54bl. Bridgeman Art Library / Royal Institution 32tr; /Chateau de Versailles /Giraudon 42tr. British Film Institute 14cr. British Library, London 16tl; 26cl. Brown Brothers 51tc. Cavendish Laboratory, Cambridge 49tr. Camera Press 43tr; 52tr; 63cb; 63cr. E. T. Archive 11c. Mary Evans Picture Library 10tl; 10br; 16bl; 18tr; 22c; 26clb; 39tc; 44tr; 44c. W. H. Freeman and Co., from Powers of Ten by Philip Morrison and the Office of Charles and Ray Eames. Copyright (c) 1982 by Scientific American Library 51br. Robert Harding Picture Library 17tl; 27bc. Michael Holford 41c. Hulton Picture Co. cover back cl; 8bl; 33cr; 38tr; 40c; 50tr; 49bl; 54br. Jet Joint Undertaking 57br. Mansell Collection 8tr; 14tl; 47bl; 48tl; 55tc. National Portrait Gallery, London 26bl. Oxford Scientific Films /Manfred Kage 38tl. Ann Ronan Picture Library cover front cr; 13tl; 13tr; 19cr; 23tr; 42c; 46tl; 46cl. Science Museum Photo Library 12bl; 15cl; 16crb; 21tl; 21tc; 21cr; 27tc; 28cr; 30cl; 34cl; 34b; 35tc; 35tr; 35br; 37tl; 51c; 56br. Science Photo Library /Brookhaven National Laboratory cover front c/James Bell 15br; /Keith Kent 19tl; /Claude Nuridsany and Maria Perendu 19bc; /Peter Manzell 23tc; /Andrew McClenaghan 39tr; /Clive Freeman 41bc; /Jeremy Burgess 43br; / J. C. Revy 45br; 47c; 58tr; 59cl; 59bl; 59tr; 59br; 62bl; /Peter Menzel 63br; /US National Archives 55tr; /Los Alamos National Laboratory 55cr; /Sandia National Laboratories 55br; /Los Alamos National Laboratory 57cl; /Barney Magrath 60tl; /Heini Schneebeli 61tr. Roger Viollet 28bl. Ullstein Bilderdienst 39c. Zefa 14tr; 29cl; 50tl; 63tr.

With the exception of the items listed above and the following: 3tl; 6-7, 11bl; 12-13, 14cr, 15tl, 15bl, 18-19, 24cl, 24bl, 24cr, 25, 28-29, 37tr, 44bc, 44t, 44tr, 45, 60tr, 61 62-63, all the photographs in this book are of objects in the collections of the Science Museum, London.